October, 1982

To Peter Liacouras,
With Best Regards
Bob Bell

WORLDS of FRIENDSHIP

SOCIOLOGICAL OBSERVATIONS

Series Editor: JOHN M. JOHNSON, *Arizona State University*

"This new series seeks its inspiration primarily from its subject matter and the nature of its observational setting. It draws on all academic disciplines and a wide variety of theoretical and methodological perspectives. The series has a commitment to substantive problems and issues and favors research and analysis which seek to blend actual observations of human actions in daily life with broader theoretical, comparative, and historical perspectives. SOCIOLOGICAL OBSERVATIONS aims to use all of our available intellectual resources to better understand all facets of human experience and the nature of our society."

—John M. Johnson

Volumes in this series:

1. **THE NUDE BEACH**, by Jack D. Douglas and Paul K. Rasmussen, with Carol Ann Flanagan
2. **SEEKING SPIRITUAL MEANING**, by Joseph Damrell
3. **THE SILENT COMMUNITY**, by Edward William Delph
4. **CROWDS AND RIOTS**, by Sam Wright
5. **THE MAD GENIUS CONTROVERSY**, by George Becker
6. **AMATEURS**, by Robert A. Stebbins
7. **CARETAKERS**, by David R. Buckholdt and Jaber F. Gubrium
8. **HARD HATS**, by Jeffrey W. Reimer
9. **LOVE AND COMMITMENT**, by Gary Schwartz and Don Merten with Fran Behan and Allyne Rosenthal
10. **OUTSIDERS IN A HEARING WORLD**, by Paul C. Higgins
11. **MOMENTUM**, by Peter Adler
12. **WORLDS OF FRIENDSHIP**, by Robert R. Bell

WORLDS of FRIENDSHIP

Robert R. Bell

SAGE PUBLICATIONS Beverly Hills London

For information address:

SAGE Publications, Inc.
275 South Beverly Drive
Beverly Hills, California 90212

SAGE Publications Ltd
28 Banner Street
London EC1Y 8QE, England

Printed in the United States of America

Library of Congress Cataloging in Publication Data

Bell, Robert R.
Worlds of friendship.

(Sociological observations ; 12)
Bibliography: p
1. Friendship. I. Title. II. Series.
BF575.F66B55 302 81-13565
ISBN 0-8039-1723-6 AACR2
ISBN 0-8039-1724-4 (pbk.)

FIRST PRINTING

CONTENTS

To Wendy,
my wife and my friend

PREFACE

Over the years sociologists have shown little interest in the study of friendship. In general, when there have been studies, the pattern has been to treat friendship as a dependent variable, as in studies of adolescence and old age.

It was through the interest and encouragement of two sociologists, Nona Glazer and Helena Lopata, that I became interested in the mid-1970s in the study of friendship. I now believe that family sociologists must start to give special recognition to friendship because it is often meeting the interpersonal needs that have traditionally been met within a marriage or family context—for example, today the many couples who live together in ways both similar and different from marriage.

This book in part reflects a careful search of the literature on friendship. There is a rich body of material by anthropologists but it focuses mostly on the unique qualities of friendships in specific cultures. For the most part in writing this book I have limited my focus to the various kinds of sociological research that is available. This book also draws upon my own study of friendship and aloneness.

I have found a very strong interest in the subject of friendship, and people typically are quite willing to discuss its meaning and implications for their lives. Certainly I am highly grateful to my respondents who were willing to reveal a great deal about their feelings. I especially thank Wendy L. Jones, of the Fox Chase Cancer Research Center (Philadelphia), for our many hours of talk about friendship.

Robert R. Bell
Philadelphia

1

MEANINGS OF FRIENDSHIP

Over the years the study of friendship has not been of great importance to sociologists. And what studies have been done tended to be limited. It was observed a number of years ago by sociologists Paul Lazarsfeld and Robert Merton that empirical studies on friendship usually focused on observed patterns rather than on the processes that give rise to those patterns.[1] That focus of study continues to appear in more current work.

Anthropologists have long had an interest in friendship. Their concern has usually been with how friendship functions in society and the part it plays in the structure of social behavior. For example, it is clear that in some societies friendship has played a very important role while in others it has been of relatively minor importance. Some societies have even seen friendship as the most holy bond of society. This idea, or ones close to it, have been expressed for centuries. Plato, Aristotle, Ovid, Cicero, St. Francis, Bacon, Montaigne, Thomas More, Descartes, Pascal, Jeremy Taylor, and Adam Smith have all written treatises on friendship, "discussing with more or less fervour the role of love and sympathy between friends in keeping society rolling."[2]

Among anthropologists friendship is often defined as an institution. But it is seen as voluntary and something to be achieved. In general, this is true only when friendship is seen as a personal and private relationship. Therefore, when friendship is recognized as a social relationship, it is a social institution in only a loose sense. Robert Paine goes on to say that in the United States friendship is a kind of institutionalized noninstitution.[3] This is in contrast with some societies where friendship is proscribed and the roles are clearly defined by Society. In those societies personal involvement is second to the institutional requirements of society.

When friendship is not a fully developed institution in society it can be linked to various other institutions. For example, close friendships can be a part of many work settings or found in various family relationships. And often within those formal institutions friendship can develop as a close and pervasive human relationship. Often within the impersonal institution friendship can provide a highly important personal dimension to at least some of the relationships.

There are certain cultural functions performed by friendship. This can be seen in the cultural features that go into its definition. First, friendship as a general relationship usually occurs within specific social class levels. This is because the general character of friendship is based on the notion of social equality. Ultimately friends must be seen as equals by one another. Second, friendship is seen as voluntaristic and highly personal. One cannot be forced to be a friend. Third, the development of friendship is based on private negotiations and is not imposed through cultural values or norms. Friendships come about because the individuals find their interpersonal exchanges to be personally rewarding.

KINSHIP

Kinship and friendship often provide the same interpersonal needs for individuals. In general, in most societies kinship has been seen as the natural and appropriate means for satisfying most interpersonal needs. Therefore, one potential area of difficulty for friendship is if it is placed in contrast or competition to kin relationships. In general, the more traditional the kinship values, the more hostile the views toward friendship. Kinship has long been believed to meet all the needs of the individual, and the individual has been expected to find with kin the kinds of emotional relationships that are associated with friendship. It has often been the case that friendship has been seen as subversive to kinship and, by its very existence, threatening the sanctity of kinship. In general, what has often happened is that friendship as a relationship of equals with warmth and feeling has been seen as unneeded and inappropriate when strong kinship existed.

This family view of friendship is reflected in the comment of a 33-year-old woman:

> I can tell at various times that my mother doesn't want to hear me talk about my friends. Especially if I mention help or advice that my friends give me she will get uptight and often say something sarcastic. What it is is that she thinks I should always turn to her. To my mother that's what families are for–not friends! She believes that just about all needs can be met within the family and to go to friends is to put down the family. My mother and I often have conflict because I don't see it that way.

In looking at the social nature of friendship we want to first look at some of the characteristics. An examination of the characteristics of friendship can provide a general definition. The most general point is that friendship is extrakin and in theory can exist with any person other than kin. This is not to say that kinship cannot involve friendship; rather, the two as social roles are mutually exclusive. Friendship refers to relationships that are entered voluntarily and are socially recognized as such by the friends and also often by others. Clearly implied is the fact of choice, and this contrasts friendship with kinship. One cannot be forced into friendship, but one has no choice over who are one's kin.

In the chapters ahead we will try to show the importance friendship has come to have in modern American society. And to a great extent this has developed because of the weakening of many kinship ties. The importance of friends is reflected in a recent national study in which respondents were asked who they would turn to first in a crisis. Slightly over half said they would turn to their friends before their families. This was true of all subgroups, although older people tend to rely more on family than do younger ones.[4]

Friendship can be seen as voluntary, close, and as an enduring social relationship. How enduring is difficult to say, but often friendships go on for many years. Most writers place great stress on the close or primary nature of friendship. Often "primary" means a strong predisposition to enter into a wide range of activities with the other person. This clearly indicates that friendship is broad and involves significantly large portions of a person's life. It is also primary because of the positive impact each friend has on the other. This usually results in the feeling of the rightness by each to make demands on the other.

As suggested, friendship carries with it rights and obligations. These are implied and vary in intensity in a friendship, but they are typically not spelled out or made explicit. To make them explicit would be to formalize the relationship and formalization is not a characteristic of American friendship. The intimacy and strength of the relationship greatly effect the rights and obligations of a friendship. But none of the emotional qualities are fixed, and so the ties of friendship are never of equal strength at all times. The strength of the friendship will vary with the respective needs of the friends over time as well as what they are putting into the taking out of the friendship at any given time.

In friendship partners are expected to treat each other as persons of real significance in their own right as well as in their relationship to each other. They are never treated as instrumental means for achieving some private end by either party. One does not "use" a friend. Furthermore, the emotional attachment to the friend rests on an appreciation of the partner's intrinsic worth. The friendship is based on *what* they are, not *who* they are. "Moreover, the personal relationship must be constantly renewed, fed by exchanges which reiterate the importance of the relationship *qua* relationship, as well as being mutually satisfying to the partners."[5]

The obligations of friendship take on a positive nature. This is because the close relationships that hold two people together do so not only through involvement and caring but also because of the obligations that each voluntarily takes on. Meeting the obligations to a friend is generally something the individual wants to do, because it is giving something to the friend—and giving is a major dimension of friendship.

Robert Brain points out that friendship needs no laws, no ceremonies, no material expectations. But in most societies love between friends is not allowed to depend on the vague bonds of moral sentiment alone. Often societies develop some social expectations associated with friendship. For example, in American society if a friend dies we *ought* to attend his funeral, but there is no obligation requiring us to do so. But in West Africa when a man dies "his best friend *must* put on filthy rags and rush into the staid atmosphere of his funeral, jeer at the weeping mourners, and tip over jars of ritual beer which have been prepared for the guests."[6]

In American society the giving by friends to one another stresses the highly positive and rewarding directions associated with friendship. Andrew Greeley talks about how friendship is an invitation: one person says to the other, "Come with me. There is nothing to fear." As a result each can enter the friendship with the belief that there is nothing to fear. Greeley says that within this context friendship is a gift. "In order that we might persuade the other to accept our invitation, we offer him an inducement, that is to say, we offer him ourself."[7]

Clearly implied in what we have said is that there is a quality of exchange between friends. While who gives what and how much relative to the other may vary between different friendships or even in a given friendship over time, it cannot be too one-sided. If the exchange were loaded too much in one direction, this would imply an inequality in the relationship. This means that on a general sociological level friendship can be described to include choice being made on a voluntary level and without any kind of coercion, as having extensive effect on each one as well as with the other. This implies many things and activities important to the persons and also a sense of binding together, a "we" feeling of having something special and private. A friendship has its own private, social dimension.

SOME PSYCHOLOGICAL QUALITIES OF FRIENDSHIP

Georg Simmel used the concept of *sociability* to describe the purest form of interaction among equal individuals. His view of sociability was that it was mutual and one person could gain only if the other person also gained.

> Sociability is the game in which one "does as if" all were equal, and at the same time, as if one honored each of them in particular. And to "do as if" is no more a lie than play or art are lies because of the deviation from reality. The game becomes a lie only when sociable action and speech are made into mere instruments of the intentions and events of practical reality–just as painting becomes a lie when it tries, in a panoramic effect, to simulate reality.[8]

People enter social relationships for many reasons and they get from their relationships a variety of results. One result may be self-confirmation: they gain a sense of who they are and something about their own self-worth. Or it may be a personal change in self-perception. Also from social relationships can come emotional expressions. "In love, in marriage, and in friendship, the expression of feeling is supposed to be the basis of the relationship between lovers, between wife and husband, between confidantes, be they two women, two men, or a woman and a man."[9]

Many people we interviewed describe in various ways the sense of self-worth they get from their friendships. For example, a 38-year-old woman said:

> My friends give me a sense of who I am. They do this by letting me express myself and sort of reflect off of them. What I mean is that I can be whoever I want to be and they let me be me. They respond in a positive way to me so I see myself in that supportive light. Often a husband or a parent won't let you be yourself. Instead, they respond to what you present by redefining you to fit their values. Good friends don't do that.

Paine observes that a basic meaning of friendship is the sense of worth one may get from it. Friendship says to the individual that someone is enjoying you, and someone understands you. But a friend can also explain you to yourself: "alternatively, a person is able to see himself in his friend."[10]

The idea that friendship implies common interests means that they share things. And a part of doing many things comes with the sharing. Furthermore, there is sometimes a strength that can be gained by individuals based on having shared with others in the past. When they encounter those who shared with them, there may be a strong sense of identification and frequently a sense of exclusiveness–exclusive because it was their private, shared experience. Friends who went through a dangerous or a very happy experience may often recall them in later interactions and draw from them not only pleasurable memories but also added strength for their ongoing relationship.

Sometimes, and over time, a close friendship can have strong impact on the personalities of the two friends. As is sometimes true of husbands and wives, this leads the individuals to become more and more like one another. Sometimes in friendship one can see clear evidence of identifications where close friends may develop similar styles in voice and gesture, dress and manner. Elizabeth Douvan points out that "a friend's knowledge and skill can represent both a resource in the relationship and a basis of attraction."[11]

When we asked people to describe what was important to friendship, their most common answer was "trust." This was because close friendships are possible only if certain barriers are eliminated and the two people can come to an understanding. This further means that what they do and get from each other is based on trust. There is usually no questioning–no wondering about the other, it is just right. This trust means that the gift of oneself to another is unselfish in terms of what is given. One does not hold back what is appropriate and natural to the friendship. The gift of oneself to the other is unselfish because there is a willingness to entrust oneself to another without any conscious holding back. However, as Greeley points out, it is not–and cannot be–unselfish in the sense that we want nothing in return. "Friendship is an exchange relation. We give ourselves because we want the other."[12]

Trust in friendship was described by a 40-year-old woman in the following way.

> The most important thing about my two very close friendships is the trust between us. I know that I can say whatever I want to to them and they won't make judgments and they won't criticize me. In fact, they will try to help me in any way they can. Furthermore I can be sure that anything I tell them will be kept to themselves. Trust in friendship to me is based on the friend not being judgmental as well as not telling anyone else.

Another woman, 45 years old, said:

> In my close friendships there is a high degree of giving and receiving. What I mean is that things that are important to each of us are expressed and reacted to by each of us. If I am really troubled and

> upset I can unload on my friends and they will understand and give serious consideration to my problems. Because we can deal with the really significant things in our lives our friendship is complete and revealing.

The capacity for intimacy varies greatly between individuals and may vary over their life cycle. Some people are more able to establish and maintain relationships with a high degree of intimacy than are others. There are also social qualities to intimacy, in that most individuals are socialized to believe certain kinds of emotional relationships are desirable and, indeed, a measure of their "healthiness" as human beings. It may be that some people feel a social necessity for intimacy rather than a strong psychologically significant need. Intimacy may be entered because it is the thing to do, not because it is what one internally needs and wants.

The notion of love is one that some find difficult to use with friendship. This is far more often the case with men than with women. For many men the notion of love between adults implies a romantic or sexual dimension. As a result, many men feel ill at ease with the notion of love related to a friend. For women, however, this is much less true: they will often describe their feelings toward a friend as love. A 37-year-old woman described her feelings:

> I love my friends. I love them just as much as I love my husband. But the love is different because it is not sexual and not romantic. The love for my friends is feeling good about them when I think of them or see them. There is usually a happiness, a delight in being together and doing things together. It's the noncompetitive and sharing qualities that are important to love. This also makes it different from anything I feel for my husband or have ever felt for any other man.

Intimacy and closeness between friends is also reflected in the values extended to friends and beliefs about friendships. In part, to say that we have a friend is to say we are not alone and that we matter to at least one other significant individual. This means that there is a person who values me and is valued by me. Furthermore, we can share some things that are important to the both of us. But along with this are the positive psychological feelings, the pleasures to be derived from friendship. There is foremost the simple pleasure that having a friend gives one the good feeling of being reaffirmed and reassured by another person.

Once a friendship has been formed, the individuals may come to see it as "natural" or inevitable that they should be friends. They come to see each other as similar and appropriate. In part this comes from the interaction they have engaged in with one another, because individuals often come to be similar in various ways with increased interaction. They may become more and more alike in their sentiments and things they like to do. "Feeling that they are similar and that the development of their friendship was 'natural' creates bonds between individuals that further the development and maintain the relationship."[13]

Friendship often suggests that each person must prove the value of his or her worthiness as a friend to the other. Friendship is not based on blind loyalty and given unquestionably. In friendship one compromises only personal convenience and efforts, not personal principles. What is clearly implied is that people have control over their destinies and that friendship is a matter of choice. Unlike with kin or in most work relationships, friends are to be chosen. As was suggested earlier, friendship grows from within and cannot be willed from the outside.

> Each of the persons entering into the relationship must desire it or it fails its true purpose. The mainspring is the pleasure derived from the sympathetic meeting of congenial minds. The area of congeniality need not be large at first, but it should be an expanding one if the relationship is to grow in strength.[14]

Friendship also often implies a willingness to forgive. But this is not forgiveness in the sense of dispensing forgiveness. Rather, it is forgiveness by accepting the friend as a unique individual. However, one does not always forgive friends for everything, and sometimes friendship may actually imply disapproval. Greeley suggests that friendship demands at times that we challenge our friends to be who and what they really are without implying in the challenge any withdrawal of our affection for them. Sometimes friendship demands that we make demands.[15]

Sometimes our friends serve as a kind of buffer or as protection from something in the world around us. For example, studies suggest that the presence of a friend, even if he does not turn away wrath and reduce physical pain, at least makes fears and anxieties tolerable. The companionship of a friend often makes people better able to endure stress- and anxiety-arousing situations. John Reisman points out that there is some scientific basis to the notion of being more effectively able to face some obstacles with a friend by your side than to do so alone.[16]

SOME SOCIAL FACTORS RELATED TO FRIENDSHIP

In general, when we choose a mate or select a friend, we choose a person very much like ourselves. Lois Verbrugge, after examining a number of studies, found that without exception adult friendships were highly homogeneous. People were alike in social and demographic characteristics as well as in attitudes, interests, intelligence, and personality traits.[17]

Similarity of age is one of the most powerful factors of friendship choice. To a great extent, social values strongly encourage the development of friendships with persons of about the same age. During childhood and adolescence the development of close friends is very much restricted to those of the same age. And because people of similar age are frequently similar also in personal and social resources, they are equal and less likely to exploit one another.

The similarity of sex is also a powerful influence on the formation of friendship (see Chapters 3 and 4). This is because often the possibility of romance or sexuality is seen as a force that may alter the friendship tie. As we will discuss in later chapters, there are many obstacles to friendship between the sexes. But there is also the attraction of friendship to the same sex because of the shared qualities of being the same sex. A 35-year-old woman said:

> There is a special quality of friendship that I feel for my women friends that I don't feel for men. It's the shared experience of having grown up as females, of knowing we share many common experiences. Because the man has always had it a bit better you often feel somewhat second class in friendships with men. If it's not sexual then it often seems to be that you are a bit patronized in the relationship.

Similar marital status is also a powerful influence on friendships. This may be an addition to the forces demanding same-sex friendship. For example, in couple friendships, the ties may be between the two wives and the two husbands (see Chapter 7). There may be both cross-sex as well as cross-marital status difficulties. A 37 year-old-man said:

> I feel much more comfortable with my new friends since I have been divorced. They are also divorced women and men. When I am around married couples I feel like they see me as a failure in marriage and therefore not quite up to their level of achievement. But when I am with my divorced friends we have that in common and it is often a very close bond between us.

Homogeneity of friendship also extends to religion. One study found that while the Jews in the sample constituted only 3 percent of the total population in the city, almost 80 percent of the friends named by Jewish men were other Jewish men. Among the Catholic men 62 percent of their friends were also Catholic men.[18]

In general, people do not limit themselves to one best friend but usually report having two or three best friends. It appears very rare for a specific friendship grouping to involve more than two people. We have found only one case of a person reporting having two friends where each of the three was equally friendly with the others as a three-person group.

A study in *Psychology Today* reported that two-thirds of the respondents said they had from one to five close friends.[19] However, at any given time as many as 25 percent of adults may report that they have *no* friends. There is also evidence that women in general report having more close friends than do men. In the chapters ahead we will try to demonstrate why women in American society today appear to have more close friends than do men.

A single friendship will not generally meet the needs of an individual throughout each person's life. New friends are added and old friends drop off. Many of a person's needs may be met in a relationship other than friendship. For example, some needs are better served by colleagues than by friends. George Levinger suggests that pair relationships are not only challenged but also nourished by the partner's other involvements.[20]

Often people like to think of their good friends as transcending time. This is often true among adults when they look back at their friendships in their youth. A feeling of nostalgia sometimes becomes linked to those old friendships and they are held to be important because they *should* be. They have existed so long, and often were initiated during a period of high romantic recall, that there is the feeling that they must be maintained. Reisman suggests that even death serves to bring true friends closer. "This concept of mythical, ideal relationships is desirable, and there are probably some who take it seriously and believe it represents reality."[21]

The kinds of friends that are needed vary over time. Norman Shulman found that the close relationships varied with changes in the life cycle and at each stage people tend to develop relationships geared to the needs and concerns they have at a particular stage of life.[22] For example, the friends of adolescence help the individual develop a sense of personal identity, while the friendships of old age may have as their primary function protecting the person from loneliness.

ACQUAINTANCES

The word "acquaintance" implies a relationship much less significant than friendship. In acquaintanceship very little is revealed about oneself. By contrast, friendship has closure with regard to the world outside and openness between the friends themselves.[23] A 33-year-old man said:

> There are many people that I like but I wouldn't call them friends. I guess acquaintances is a better description. These are people that I see and do certain things with. Like some of the people I work with. We pass the time of day and joke around. But we never get personal in any way. I think that is probably the way all of us want to keep it. I have had acquaintances push a little and get too personal. I haven't liked it and quickly backed off.

Paine argues that acquaintanceship has a structure that not only stops short of friendship but in several respects is also opposed to it. He says that acquaintances cannot be friends (as can spouses, for example). "Indeed, an important aspect of acquaintanceship may be phrased as the problem of controlling and curbing approaches to intimacy."[24]

Ordinarily, then, acquaintanceship is not a relationship of intimacy or exchange of confidences. However, a great amount of information may be passed between those who are acquaintances. But there is little elaboration as to any code of conduct, and typically the relationship is a surface one. Paine suggests that an important problem of acquaintanceship may be controlling approaches to intimacy. "Thus a feature of acquaintanceship is its mediation by other relationships that are outside it. It is also unlike friendship in that it is unaffected when extended to include several or many persons."[25]

Simmel suggested that acquaintanceship does not indicate knowledge of one about the other and involves no actual insight into the personality of the other. For Simmel, acquaintanceship depended upon the knowledge of the *that* of the personality, not of its *what.*

> After all, by saying that one is acquainted, even well acquainted, with a particular person, one characterizes quite clearly the lack of really intimate relations. Under the rubric of acquaintance, one knows of the other only what he is toward the outside, either in the purely social-representative sense or in the sense of that which he shows us.[26]

THE ENDING OF FRIENDSHIP

Implied in friendship is symmetry or balance—that there be equality on both sides. This means that each friend gets and gives pretty much the same. Of course, there can be wide variations for short periods of time, but if that continues, the balance is lost and inequality characterizes the relationship. Once inequality enters, the potential for breakup becomes strong.

There is always the potential for conflict in a friendship when both persons desire some of the same things. One of the major values of friendship is that each have a concern for the identity of the other. Each wants to help the other maintain a high sense of personal worth. Therefore, sometimes norms develop in a friendship to help avoid or minimize possible embarrassment. For example, this can happen if one friend achieves or gets something the other would also have liked to achieve. John Hepburn suggests two norms which help prevent conflict from occurring. One would be to avoid the other's sensitive zones. For example, if that person would have liked something and feels bad about not achieving it, it is not brought up. Another norm is that if one gets something the other would have liked but didn't get, the winner presents his or her achievements as attributable to luck or somewhat greater experience. To remain unstated is that the other was unsuccessful for any reason of incompetency or ineptness.[27]

Lazarsfeld and Merton found that close friendships that can tolerate a conflict of values without the relationship being severely threatened are probably the ones least subject to such conflict. This is because friends are strongly motivated to ease their value differences in the hopes of easing any strain. So in the give and take of friendship the divergence of values tend, to be reduced. If the friends have an approximately equal emotional stake in the relationship, this is likely to occur through mutual accommodations of their values. "If one is more deeply involved in the relationship than the other, his values are more likely to be motivated to accord with the values of the less deeply involved. Presumably, if this self-corrective process did not occur, then close friendships would be even harder to come by and to maintain than they apparently are."[28]

Often friendships last because the people want them to and not because there are intrinsic positive reasons for continuing. Thus, the measure of the goodness of friendship is determined by what the person feels for it, not by simply that some arbitrary requirement of having lasted a prescribed amount of time has been met. But sometimes friendships are maintained simply because they have existed for a long time.

Friendships can be ended by external forces that drive the friends apart. But whatever the causal origins, friendships are ultimately broken from inside the relationship, not from outside it. Furthermore, as Paine observes, any attempt by friends to make an explicit statement about what their friendship *should* be (in order to save) will probably only hasten its demise.[29] To work consciously to save a friendship, like trying to save a marriage, usually is not very successful.

Ultimately the making and the breaking of friendships in our society is mainly a matter of personal choice, which is generally beyond social control. Further, the content of a friendship cannot be at all accurately determined from a position outside it, while friends themselves are unlikely to be able to predict the course their friendship will take, length.[30] Given the importance of spontaneity and equality to friendship, predictability is greatly reduced. Therefore, the more dynamic and changing the friendship, the less the chance of knowing where it is going. The more innovative the friendship, the more possible directions it may take.

Whatever the reasons, all friendships must ultimately come to an end. If they continue without interpersonal breakdown, they end with the death of one of the friends. However, long after death the friends may remain highly significant in the memory of the survivor. On the level of living friendships, Greeley has pointed out that the most depressing part of the friendship game is that one can lose. But if we are not willing to run risks, we will never have friends. Friendship can only occur when we offer ourselves to the other, and to offer oneself to someone else is the most risky of all human endeavors.[31]

Friendships are entered into voluntarily and can be left in the same way. But friendships can also be entered for a variety of reasons and left for many causes. Sometimes the terminations of friendships may be more highly charged than was the friendship. The emotional costs of ending a friendship have more often been dealt with in poetry, fiction, and philosophy than in scientific terms. The high level of emotion in ending a friendship is similar to what often occurs when a marriage ends. Yet friendships, like marriages, sometimes do not have emotion-charged endings but simply drift apart.

Over time, because friendships are subject to private negotiations, persons may break their friendships, revise them, or simply drift away from one another. "Losing a friend may be painful but it is also an option that can be taken without consultation or an official change in status; being an ex-friend is not a publicly recognized status, as is so often the case when a person severs any other type of affiliation."[32] To be an ex-friend would often seem to imply not a neutral role but a negative one. If one is no longer considered a friend, this usually implies that one has failed in some way—in a way that made what was good and satisfactory no longer so. In a range of relationships from positive to negative, the ex-friend would clearly be toward the negative side.

Kurth has observed that while we may drift in and out of friendly relations, we do not do the same with friendships. Friendships are believed to be lasting and not something one dabbles in. Many friendships are maintained even though one or both of the individuals feels he or she would like to dissolve it. But to dissolve it is to take a drastic step many are not willing to make. So often we continue with an eye on the day when we can find a painless and graceful way to become less involved and end the friendship.[33]

Over time friendships are subjected to various influences. They may be affected by changes for one of the persons. For example, often a friendship may be ended because one person gets married and comes to feel the old friendship is no longer appropriate. Or close friendships may be accelerated by a personal crisis of one of the individuals who turns to their friend in a new and more needing way. When the other person responds, he or she becomes reciprocally involved and the friendship becomes more intense. What allows good friendship to survive many external influences is that it generally can absorb the more transient feelings of anger, resentment, or disappointment. Friendship makes it possible for people to tolerate the falling short of original hopes and to readjust to new problems that might arise. Good friendship can also tolerate prosperity, "with its double-edged threat and promise of greater autonomy and independence for each member of the friendship, because such freedom always hints at the greater possibility of separation and loss; they may need each other less than before, which is not likely to be felt as an unmitigated gain."[34]

THE FRIENDSHIP INTERVIEWS

Beginning in 1976 and continuing through 1980 I conducted interviews with 101 women and 65 men. My study design was simple and in no sense represents any kind of systematically selected sample. I started out by interviewing women and men I knew—in fact, some were my friends. With time I included a wide variety of people, but none of them was a complete stranger to me. Everyone I interviewed I had talked to socially or professionally for a minimum of two or three hours before I asked if I could interview them.

My purpose in the interviews was to explore and learn from my respondents their views and experiences with and about friendship and aloneness. In this book only a little is said about aloneness and loneliness (I am at present writing a book in those areas). My interviews were structured, in that I knew what kinds of questions I was going to ask. Generally, once the question was asked, I would encourage as much elaboration as the person wanted to give. I took extensive notes during the interview, which never lasted less than one hour and in some cases as long as five hours—the average interview lasted about two hours.

With few exceptions I found my respondents interests in friendship very strong, and friendship played an important part in their lives. The respondents are a selective group because they are mostly the kinds of people who greatly value friendship. For the most part they are well educated and middle or upper-middle class. Except for those in higher education, almost all others, both women and men, had full-time careers.

THE CHAPTERS AHEAD

It is clear that friendship has undergone and continues to undergo change in America. One indication of this is the difficulty in defining friendship, because there are many kinds of relationships in which "friend" may be applied. It would also appear that friendship is becoming increasingly important in American society. Certainly as the emotional ties and rewards through the family are reduced other relationships are needed. There is also evidence that friendship is becoming of greater importance at all stages of life. In the chapters ahead I will examine how friendship has changed and its importance at different ages and marital statuses during the life cycle.

In Chapter 2 the interest is first in childhood as a socialization experience for the child. With children more involved in schools at younger ages than in the past, the kinds of relationships they develop are basic to their development. Also in this chapter is an examination of the crucial nature of friendship for adolescents as they move through the transition from child to adult.

In Chapters 3 and 4 the concern is with friendship among women and among men. It is argued that friendship has come to take on increasing importance for women, mainly because open and revealing friendships across sex lines have been difficult and often impossible. The main focus in examining friendships between men is that their socialization against revealing emotions often prevents psychological depth.

Chapter 5, on cross-sex friendships, looks at the problems that make friendship between women and men difficult. The major problem is the social assumption of romance and sexuality, seen as an inevitable development in most cross-sex relationships.

The interest in Chapter 6 is with friendships between wives and husbands and how married couples react to various types of friendships the other may have. It also appears that marriages are meeting fewer and fewer needs of interpersonal relationships, reflected in the high rate of interpersonal disillusionment with marriage. There is some evidence that friendships for many young people are a kind of alternative to marriage. Many choose to live together without marriage and without permanent commitment. What may be a pattern of future friendship could be shorter-term relationships with different people over the years.

Chapter 7 examines the nature of friendships that develop among married couples. In general, each partner may have some of his or her own friends, and those friends are not significantly shared with the spouse. But the couple will typically have other couples as friends. The common pattern is for the friendship to be between the four people or along sex lines, wife to wife and husband to husband. With married couples it is relatively rare for the friendships to be two-person and across sex lines.

It is argued in Chapter 8 that friendship has come to be increasingly important to divorced people. Emotional breakups create the need for another who can meet interpersonal needs. The result is more often a friend than a relative. Possibly the most important contribution friends make to the divorced persons is in helping them adjust and adapt to their new role. Often the new friends are themselves divorced.

Chapter 9 looks at the role of friendship for elderly people. This is often a period of decreasing friend involvement because of retirement and the death of friends. Because of the much greater life expectancy of women, many of them are confronted with widowhood for a number of years, and for them friendship has come to be of increasingly greater importance.

NOTES

1. Lazarsfeld, Paul F. and Robert K. Merton, "Friendship as a Social Process: A Substantive and Methodological Analysis," in *Freedom and Control in Modern Society,* M. Berger, T. Abel, and C. H. Page, eds. (New York: Octogon Books, 1954), p. 25.
2. Brain, Robert, *Friends and Lovers* (New York: Basic Books, 1976), p. 12.
3. Paine, Robert, "In Search of Friendship: An Exploratory Analysis in 'Middle-Class' Culture," *Man,* December 1969, p. 514.
4. Parlee, Mary Brown, "The Friendship Bond," *Psychology Today,* October 1979, p. 54.
5. Glazer-Melbin, Nona, *Old Family/New Family: Interpersonal Relationships* (New York: D. Van Nostrand Co., 1975), p. 50.
6. Brain, *Friends and Lovers,* pp. 17-18.
7. Greeley, Andrew, *The FriendshipGame* (New York: Doubleday, 1971), p. 29.

8. Simmel, Georg, *The Sociology of Georg Simmel,* trans. Kurt H. Wolff (Free Press, 1950), p. 49.

9. Glazer-Melbin, (New York: p. 5. *Old Family/New Family,* p. 5.

10. Paine, "In Search of Friendship," p. 517.

11. Douvan, Elizabeth, "Interpersonal Relationships: Some Questions and Observations," in *Close Relationships,* G. Levinger and H. L. Raush, eds. (Amherst: University of Massachusetts Press, 1977), p. 19.

12. Greeley, *The Friendship Game,* p. 40.

13. Kurth, Suzanne B., "Friendships and Friendly Relations," in *Social Relationships,* G. J. McColl, ed. (Chicago: Aldine, 1970), p. 157.

14. Wood, Margaret M., *The Stranger: A Study in Social Relationships* (New York: Columbia University Press, 1934), p. 46.

15. Greeley, p. 92.

16. Reisman, John M., *Anatomy of Friendship* (New York: Irvington Publishers, 1979), p. 201.

17. Verbrugge, Lois M., "The Structure of Adult Friendship Choices," *Social Forces,* December 1977, p. 577.

18. Rubin, Zick, *Liking and Loving,* New York: Holt, Rinehart & Winston, 1973), pp. 136-37.

19. Parlee, "The Friendship Bond," p. 45.

20. Levinger, George, "The Embrance of Lives: Changing and Unchanging," in *Close Relationships,* G. Levinger and H. L. Rausch, eds. (Amherst: University of Massachusetts Press, 1977), pp. 11-12.

21. Reisman, *Anatomy of Friendship,* p. 111.

22. Shulman, Norman, "Life-Cycle Variations in Patterns of Close Relationships," *Journal of Marriage and the Family,* November 1975, p. 820.

23. Paine, p. 130.

24. Ibid., p. 129.

25. Ibid., p. 115.

26. Simmel, *Sociology of George Simmel,* p. 320.

27. Hepburn, John R., "Violent Behavior in Interpersonal Relationships," *The Sociological Quarterly,* Summer 1973, p. 431.

28. Lazarsfeld and Merton, "Friendship as a Social Process," p. 35.

29. Paine, p. 512.

30. Ibid., p. 514.

31. Greeley, p. 17.

32. Suttles, Gerald D., "Friendship as a Social Institution," in *Social Relationships,* G. J. McColl, ed. (Chicago: Aldine, 1970), p. 97.

33. Kurth, "Friendships and Friendly Relations," p. 158.

34. Holmes, Donald J., *Psychotherapy* (Boston: Little, Brown, 1972), p. 361.

2

CHILDHOOD AND ADOLESCENT FRIENDSHIPS

The child enters life with the potential for social growth, and social interaction with others becomes a necessary condition. The biological necessities are that no severe mental handicaps exist and that sufficient time pass for physical maturation to take place. Initially, most infants learn their basic social skills within the family setting. As they develop the skills to relate to their family, they are also learning skills that will be used in other kinds of social interaction, including friendship. In this chapter we first examine how and what kinds of skills develop for friendship during infancy and childhood. Second, we will look at the direction and meaning friendship takes during adolescence.

CHILDHOOD

Generally, during the first year of life not much of infants' behavior can truly be described as social. Their interaction with adults is usually heavily one-way, with most that is social coming from adults. During the first year any contact with other infants or children can barely be described as social in the sense of friendship. But in the early months of their second year of life young children begin to direct what is clearly social behavior toward other children of about the same age. "These behaviors can be most clearly identified by the fact that the toddler looks at the other while smiling, extending an object, or making sounds."[1]

Initially, it appears that when young children interact it is in a one-to-one relationship rather than in larger groups. Rubin found that during the first two years of life, when children did interact, they did so in twosomes and almost never in groups of three or more. However, by ages three and four changes in the size of their groups did occur. "Although nursery school children still spend much of their time in pairs, they begin to play in larger groups and to become concerned with group belonging."[2]

It seems clear that many children between the ages of two and three have developed paired relationships that are of a voluntary nature. In other words, they show a preference for certain persons around them, and this appears to be true both for girls and boys. DuBois found that groups of playmates, all within limited age ranges, seem to develop in all societies. The playmates appear to develop a prototype of casual friendship; this relationship is characterized by shifting pairs. But often those kinds of relationships common to the very young are not valued by adults. DuBois observed that "in no society so far examined do adults prize highly the childhood playmate relationship, even though parents may be indulgent and hospitable toward their children's play fellows."[3]

Parents are highly influential in their children's development of values about friendships. They are important because they are the most significant others in the lives of their children during at least the first few years. And the very young often pick up cues from their parents about age peers they should become friendly with. But even at young ages children often play the major part in their friendship choices. Rubin states that the most central basis for the development of toddlers' friendships is "probably the existence of similarities between their development levels, temperaments, and behavior styles."[4]

There appears to be what might reasonably be defined as friendships developing at about the age of three. Although at that age, when children are together, some may be more interested in doing things alone or even daydreaming than interacting with other children. But for many, by age three friendships become important in their lives. Friendships come to occupy, both in actual conduct and in the world of thought and fantasy, a large portion of the child's waking hours.[5] By the age of three there seems little doubt that children are responding positively to at least some of their peer relationships. There is also some evidence that children at this age who lack peer relationships may suffer to some extent and strive to compensate through fantasy for what they do not have in reality.[6] For some, this may mean the development of imaginary friends. However, we have found that relatively few adults—at least as they recall—ever had imaginary friends.

Children between three to five characteristically view as friends those who are their playmates at any given time. That is, whoever they are playing with on a given occasion they will say are their friends. And while young children may have some enduring relationships with others, they typically conceive of these in terms of momentary interaction. Selman and Selman describe the friendship stage of those from ages three to seven as that of "momentary playmateship." This stage is described as one in which the child has difficulty distinguishing between a physical action, such as grabbing a toy, and the psychological intention behind the action. "Friends are valued for their material and physical attributes, and defined by proximity. As one child told us, 'He is my friend! 'Why?' 'He has a giant Superman doll and a real swing set!' "[7]

During the early years much is learned about social relationships, and there is often uncertainty and gaps in knowledge as to what should be done under various circumstances. Also involved is a necessity for moving outside the self and taking into consideration the other. Because the young child's world has been so egocentric, this is frequently a difficult thing to do. As a result, relationships with other children often involve negative feelings. One of the characteristics of friendships among the young is a great deal of quarreling. Very often the negative feelings disappear after a short period of time. While it is common for young children to have what appear to be bitter fights and arguments, when those occur the children very often appear to be friends again a few hours later.

Sometimes children will define another as a friend for what he or she does not do. Often the friend is a child who does not hurt, tease, or try to take advantage of the other. "If children make fun, those who don't join in the ridicule are apt to be seen as their friends. If a child from their school says 'hello' on the street, the child will probably be regarded by them as a friend."[8]

Children at young ages are affected in their friendship choices by adult values in many different ways. Parents and teachers often pass on to children values about beauty or attractiveness. By the time they are in nursery school children usually have learned who is good looking and who is not. For the child defined in these positive terms there are many benefits. Preschoolers who have good looks are more popular and better liked by their peers. By contrast, the child who is unattractive is not only not selected as a friend but may be confronted with why he or she is being rejected. The other children may say he or she is fat or ugly. Adults may also contribute in a variety of ways. For example, "adults who see attractive children misbehave are more likely to assume there is valid justification for their acts."[9] The unattractive child, on the other hand, is more likely to be seen as deserving of punishment.

In friendships among adults sex differences are a significant barrier to a close relationship. Some sex discrimination appears among young children. In general, before age two there is little evidence of sex preference in children's play. Members of the opposite sex are chosen as playmates about as often as members of the same sex. But from ages three and four there emerge new patterns of sex composition, and both boys and girls come to prefer their own sex as playmates. At those young ages children are becoming responsive to the values of their peers, and one of the strongest early values is to associate with one's own sex. By the time children reach age ten, sex segregation is almost complete. Parents also play a part in teaching their children sex segregation in friendship choice. Rubin found that even before children entered nursery school their parents sought same-sex playmates for them and encouraged "sex-appropriate" activities.[10]

Children are very much like adults in the number of close friends they see themselves as having. Children tend to name one or two close friends and generally not more than five. Often these friendships that are made in childhood remain for many years. Reisman observes that it is surprising how stable some of the close friendships of childhood are, given especially high value and thought to be "extra special" because they come from childhood. As a result, a special effort is often made to make sure they are continued.[11] The fact that they have lasted for a long time may become the major reason for their continuation.

One of the most difficult lessons children must learn is to get outside themselves in their relationships to others. They must give up some of their egocentrism and enter a give and take relationship with another person. It is not surprising that at first children look at friendship in a one-sided and egocentric fashion. They look at the friend in terms of what he or she can do for them. "A friend is a friend because 'I like him' or 'he plays with me' or 'I want him to be my friend.' " Only at later stages do children become capable of figuratively standing back and taking the other person's viewpoint."[12]

Often when children are asked to describe what they like about their friends, they tend to concentrate on physical characteristics and activities. They look at what they can see rather than what they might feel. " 'Andy's got red hair and he always wears cowboy boots.' As children grow older they begin to supplement such concrete descriptions with abstract concepts that refer to behavioral dispositions, 'He's a big show off.' "[13]

When young children develop new patterns with their first playmates they are entering the world of their peers and taking themselves, for periods of time, from the adult world where they have been physically and socially inferior. This means that they must learn to relate to others as equals, and their new playmates provide them with a way to compare themselves with others the same age. They learn what it is like to be a three- or four-year-old by seeing that behavior in others. It also provides them with the means of making comparisons in their development. They learn how well they do things as compared to others their age. If they are behind in some areas, this often serves as a spur to development.

It can be argued that at no time in life are friends more important than during childhood. This is because not only is the child learning so much that is new, but other children provide him or her with the means of learning a great deal about him/herself. Therefore, a major function of childhood friends, whether intended or not, is encouraging development of the child. "Friends help children to separate from parents and expose them to a wider reference group than the family, a broader range of values, living arrangements and beliefs."[14]

As children become more involved with other children, they break away from some of their dependence on their parents. During the first, second, and third grades, children change from preferring the company of their parents to the company of their peers, but this appears to occur gradually. At the same time that children are differentiating friends from family, they are also beginning to differentiate between friends. They come to see some friends as closer than others. Friends come to serve central functions for children that parents do not, and they play a crucial role in shaping children's social skills and sense of identity.

It is during early childhood that many children first experience loneliness. Certainly, many children are not successful in developing friendships or in having as many friendships as they would like to have. And often children anxiously look toward others to escape loneliness. But it is also during childhood that some children begin to develop positive values about aloneness. This means feeling good about being alone some of the time. A 26-year-old woman, describing her childhood, said:

> When I was young people would come over to my house because I was a good listener and not a talker. I used to often wish they would leave me alone. I often preferred to be alone and I would separate myself from them even when they were there. I would just tune them out, but they would keep coming over because I was a good listener. They would think of me as a good friend because they told me so much about themselves. But they never seemed to be aware that I didn't tell them much about myself–that all I really wanted was to be left alone.

One young woman, 20 years old, described the fantasies of her childhood this way:

> In childhood I had a lot of fantasies, I had imaginary friends. We used to make up plays. I would daydream and act out in my mind what I wanted to do when I grew up. I would arrange people in roles and have them act out a play. These were people I knew, but not friends. Up until I was about twelve I had no interest in real friends. I liked to know a lot of people so I could use them in my dreams. In that way they would be the cooperative friends I wanted, where in reality they never would have been.

Rubin argues that children's groups take on their greatest importance during late childhood—the years between about nine and twelve. "At a time when children must leave the safety of the family, a group of friends can play a valuable supportive role, especially in the domains of sexual and emotional development."[15] This is also because their peers are a part of this learning experience of new kinds of emotional development. The young are very dependent on each other as sources of learning.

The period of late childhood is one of continued great learning. At this time children have learned only a limited amount about the world and the people around them. Therefore, the level of complexity or sophistication they have will not be great. Often the friendships of preadolescents are likely to be naive and not very profound or reflective. In part this is because the boundaries of the self and those of friends are not as yet clearly drawn. "One does not know when one is being too intimate or too standoffish, because one is too self-centered."[16]

Many American children grow up in highly mobile families—some changing their place of residence every few years. This can make friendships difficult: every move means ending relationships starting all over in new neighborhoods and in new schools. Entering a new setting can result in feelings of not belonging and of loneliness. A 25-year-old woman described part of her childhood as follows.

> My father was an army officer and we moved around a lot. So every time we moved there would be a distinct period of loneliness. I was an only child so there were many times when I was alone and lonely until I could make new friends. About the time I developed some new friends we moved again. I think because of this I never really developed the ability to make good and close friends. I know that I have never had any really close friends and those I have had have not lasted for long periods.

As suggested, initially for the child friendships have no profound purpose or great depth. Initially, when we are very young, we probably take our friends for granted. Our friends are there to amuse us, have fun with, share secrets and confidences with, and to provide us with a feeling of popularity. It is only as we get older that our friends take on meaning. Rubin found that the friendships of preschool children had a variety of functions. Friends give security, standards against which to measure oneself and partners with whom to do things. Friends during this period are also "guides to unfamiliar places, and apprentices who confirm one's own developing sense of competence and expertise."[17]

As I shall show in later chapters, there is evidence that for many adults there is a close relationship between their ability to develop strong friendships and their ability to deal well with solitary situations. It may be that the personal resources that help make friends are essentially the same as those that allow the person to deal with the world on his or her own. It has also been observed that among children those with the strongest friendships not only socialize better in a group but also spend more time in solitary and constructive activity. "Their trust in the stability of the relationship favors independent actions and obviates activities."[18]

For many adults, especially teachers, there is a contradiction in children being involved in their groups and also being encouraged to develop solitary behavior. Often in the classroom there is such a strong commitment to the importance of relating to others that children who prefer to spend a good deal of time by themselves are likely to be regarded as having a problem. "With a passion for popularity comes a tendency to conform to peer-group standards that can undermine much else that is of value in children's lives, including individual skills, tastes, ideals and commitments."[19]

Because of the egocentric nature of children's personalities, it is not surprising that what is often of most importance about friends is what the friends can give them. One study reported that about half the children mentioned that friends were helpful in some way when they were asked what they liked about their friendships. And this number gradually increased into the adult years, where the great majority of adults seemed to expect their friends to serve them in some useful way.[20]

Distinctions about friends by children of different ages are often made. Younger children in their preteen years are most likely to describe their friends as playmates and helpers. For them, a friend is one who plays with you and helps you. By contrast, older children more often mention friends as confidantes. For them, a friend is someone you can trust with secrets and problems. As one gets older the mental and emotional exchanges become of greatest importance.

Expectations having to do with pleasure are mentioned far more often by younger children than by adults. Reisman reports that the great majority of youngsters claimed they liked having a friend because of some activity related to play. "By the age of ten or eleven years, pleasure becomes less often mentioned, and in adulthood, perhaps only one in three depicts the joys of friendship in terms of golfing companions or card playing chums."[21]

The learning experiences of childhood are not always positive. Many early socialization experiences children go through are the learning of things they should not or cannot do. Through their relationships with other children they learn not only how to get along but also how *not* to get along. There may also be some undesirable effects of friendship. "Intimate friendships give rise not only to self acceptance, trust and rapport, but also to insecurity, jealousy, and resentment."[22] Friendship can force on the child qualities that are not always defined as desirable.

The Selmans observe that from about age six to twelve the child develops the ability to see interpersonal perspectives as reciprocal and where each person must begin to pay attention to the other's perspective. At this stage friendship includes a concern for what each person thinks about the other. It becomes more of a two-way street. Friendship is seen as not working unless both friends participate. "However, the limitations of this stage is that the child still sees the basic purpose of friendship as serving many separate self-interests, rather than mutual interests."[23] They are still—at least in part—living in their egocentric worlds.

As was suggested earlier, childhood places heavy stress on similarity and conformity in friendships. Many studies document the tendency for pairs of friends to be approximately the same age, the same sex, the same size, the same level of intelligence, and the same degree of physical maturity.[24] These factors make for a high level of conformity not only in who are friends but also in how they behave in friendship. Friendship groups contribute to their members' similarities. Typically, there is strong pressure on children to conform to the expectations and standards of their peer groups. As a result, the friends tend to be very much alike.

The sex differences in friendship emerge and solidify during childhood. Many of the characteristics that distinguish friendship between the sexes and within each sex are well established during this period and continue through the adult years. There is some evidence that the need for intimate friendship arises earlier for girls than for boys, and that girls' friendships are generally more emotional than those of boys. This is largely a reflection of girls developing relationships with one other girl, while boys are more likely to be involved in broader, but less emotional, group activities.

Another study suggests that girls, more than boys, use their sex peers as their most important reference group at younger ages. This may be due to girls having a more difficult time than boys separating themselves from home. Parents generally hold on longer to daughters than they do to sons. Also, girls mature faster than boys and go through more striking physical changes.

Girls are also freer than boys to express feelings, lean on friends, and show affection. "Many, many boys are still bugged by the fear that to be close to a male friend is something akin to homosexuality."[25]

Clearly, the most crucial difference between girls and boys is that girls tend to interact in small groups, particularly dyads, while boys tend to interact in larger groups. It has been argued that many game requirements boys go through initially encourage them to develop nonexclusive friendships. And once those kinds of friendships are developed, they become the pattern for the continued tendency for boys to interact in large groups. By contrast, "the development of exclusive friendships in girls furthers their tendency to interact in dyads and leads to the development of other types of social skills, such as the ability to engage in intimate self-disclosure."[26]

A 38-year-old man describes the kind of friendship he remembers as a boy.

> When I think about growing up I don't remember any special friends. Instead, on the street where I grew up there were seven of us about the same age and we did things together. Sometimes all of us, but more often any combination of the seven of us. It wasn't really a gang and didn't have any real leader. You never really thought of doing something with a friend but rather with the guys.

Often boys tend to see the group as an entity and, when asked about values, stress loyalty and solidarity. Girls more often value the intimacy of the two-person friendship.

Basically, two explanations can be offered for the fact that girls' and boys' patterns of social interaction occur in different-sized groups. First is the difference in the number of participants in boys' and girls' games. Boys are more often involved in activities that call for large groups. Second, girls tend to engage in more intimate behavior than do boys, and their two-person friendships are most appropriate for intimate behavior.[27]

Rubin suggests that girls may have a more acute appreciation than do boys of the fragile nature of intimate friendships and of the ways in which friendship may threaten another. This is reflected in the strong resistance to expanding a friendship to include a third person, as well as the tendency for girls to keep their two-person friendships separate from one another.[28] Boys are much less concerned with the emotional interchange in their groups and more concerned with the dominance hierarchies of their groups. They are also more concerned with how they are able to fit their individual skills and abilities with those of other boys.

For boys, there is often a competitive aspect of their friendship which is much less common for girls. When girls get together in groups, the tone of their relationships is more likely to be of intimacy than of rebellion. There is some evidence that friendships among boys tend to be more lasting and stable than those of girls. The stability may result from the lower degree of intensity and consequent reduced chance for conflict. "Boys rely on their peers for support in fulfilling needs for independence and achievement. Girls use them for the development of interpersonal skills and close relationships with one or two others."[29]

In the chapters ahead I will examine in more detail some of the skills and directions of personality development that occur for many girls as a result of their friendships. Girls, in their intimate relationships of childhood, develop an aptitude for nurturance and emotional expression. They also develop the social skills that are basic to interpersonal relationships they will utilize over the rest of their lives. Boys very often develop skills that will help them in the traditional male work world they will enter in the future. In their larger groups boys learn to operate in systems of rules and to get along with people they may not especially like. These are social skills that are highly relevant to modern organizational structures.

As children get older, a part of what segregates them by sex are the romantic overtones of boy-girl relationships. As they enter late childhood and move into their preteen years their interaction becomes especially strained. This represents an awareness of each other that in many instances replaces the indifference of the previous few years about the opposite sex. In the preteen years they move into tentative, uncertain relationships that cross sex lines. The romantic dimension brings on a self-consciousness which was not the pattern with same-sex friends. As a result, it is often difficult for them to develop relaxed relationships with one another.

In general, at probably all ages boys are less aware of and interested in girls than girls are in boys. This is because traditionally even young girls are made more aware of the importance of the opposite sex to their futures. This is also reflected in the finding that the proportion of girls choosing a friend of the opposite sex is higher at all ages than that of boys. In general this tendency increases with age.[30] At all ages females appear to have more interest in opposite sex friends than do males.

ADOLESCENT FRIENDSHIPS

From the time infants take their first step, they are literally and figuratively moving away from their parents. A major characteristic of childhood is the movement for independence, and in the adolescent years this accelerates at a rapid rate. Adolescence comprises the transition years between childhood and adulthood. And to reach adult recognition in society one must leave behind the dependencies of childhood. One of the characteristics is that during adolescence the ties of the family typically become less important. Instead of the family their relationships with their peers take on increasing significance. As a result the strong dependency typical of the family comes to be distributed in the new nonkin relationships.

Anthropologist Cora DuBois writes that adolescence appears in all societies to be the time during which nonfamily gregariousness, particularly that of friendships, acquires the greatest emotional urgency for the individual.[31] The social system also contributes to many of the close relationships of peers. Adolescents and young adults tend to be involved in nonfamily activities such as education, the development of careers, and mate selection. This means they must be more involved with people of similar age who have similar concerns.[32]

As was suggested, because adolescence is a period of transition, much experience is new and therefore has created a great deal of uncertainty. Various studies have shown a strong reluctance in adolescents to be seen as different from their peers. One study reports that when adolescents were asked to make a variety of choices, they chose what they believed their peers would choose. "Adolescents, perceiving themselves to be more like peers in regard to tastes in clothes and in regard to feelings about school, find peer-favored alternatives in these areas psychologically closer and more acceptable."[33]

Adolescents' shift from family to peer influences is not easily accepted by the family. As a result, the competition between parents and peers to influence the adolescent often intensifies as he or she moves through the years of adolescence. Involvement in romantic relationships is often a means of asserting independence from the family. One writer suggests: "It may be that the adolescent male's assertion of independence from the family occurs increasingly through his relationships with the adolescent girl friends whom his parents disapprove of rather than through his relationships with an adolescent male peer group whom his parents approve of."[34]

One study found that both males' and females' peer group involvement and orientation increased as they moved through school until the tenth grade. At that time there was a leveling off for males and a reduction in peer orientation for females. It was also found that females have tended to "peak" in terms of degree of peer orientation at an earlier age-grade level than was the case for males.[35]

The quality of friendships during adolescence is often quite different from that of childhood. Sommer says that before puberty friendships are relatively unemotional and lack the complex love-hate extensions which sometimes characterize family relationships. "In early adolescence some friendships remain superficial. Others, while perhaps short lived, are very intense."[36] The Selmans write that by early adolescence the young person can step outside a friendship and view it from a generalized third-person perspective. A shift occurs which allows them to see friendhips not as reciprocal cooperation for each person's self-interest, but as collaboration with others for mutual and common interests. "Friends share feelings, help each other to resolve personal and interpersonal conflicts, and help each other solve personal problems."[37]

Because so much of what adolescents do and who they do it with is new, there may be insecurities associated with the rapid social change. Similarity of age is a powerful force for conformity during this time, and an age difference of a year or two may be seen as too extreme for a close friendship. Often when an adolescent chooses someone older as a friend, he or she enters into a somewhat different relationship. Kon observes that "the orientation toward a person of the same age conveys a striving for more or less equal relationships. The selection of an older friend expresses a need for a model, for authority, for guidance."[38]

Another study found that the closer the friend, the higher the chronological age correlation. The girls in the study tended to choose as friends other girls of similar age and degrees of dominance and sociability. "The degree of emotional stability, self-sufficiency, introversion, and self-confidence seems to have little to do with the formation of friendships among adolescent girls."[39] This suggests that, with few exceptions, all kinds of personalities are able to develop friendships—it is *not* that only some types of personalities are able to develop friendships.

During adolescence many hours are spent in educational institutions. Secondary schools are more than just places to be educated. They are also major centers of social development for adolescents. It is in the school that many friendships develop and are maintained. Furthermore, the values that one's friends have about school greatly influence the individual. For example, the educational aspirations and attainments of a person's friends strongly influences his or her own aspirations and achievements.[40] Because peers have more influence often than either parents or teachers, the peer values about education are of great importance. If one's friends value education, the individual usually will also.

One study of adolescents found that close friendships represented a relationship between the subject and a peer whose common interests and values range from the intermittently personal to the very personal. The social intimacy between the adolescent friends was a personal relationship that expressed itself in self-disclosure and trust. This tended to intensify the solidarity between the friends and to isolate them from others. "Closest friendship and social intimacy intersect when the principals confide and share private experiences."[41] While in early adolescence, as in childhood, individuals still want friends who are useful, they also increasingly want friends who can help them deal with social and personal problems.

The transitional nature of adolescence also means that one of the most important psychological functions of friendship is the positive support it can give to self-image and self-esteem. Fellow adolescents also often provide a receptive and enthusiastic audience for the testing of ideas that adults might find tiresome or presumptuous. Furthermore, out of the friendship comes verification of who the friends are. There is also status, affection, security, and acceptance. These are all highly valued interpersonal rewards to receive from friends at all ages, but they are especially important during adolescence because this is the first time they are developed with depth and complexity.

The intimacy of adolescent friendships also becomes the way individuals can find in their friends a sounding board against which to project uncertainties, explorations, and defeats. Grievances and victories are also presented before others who are in essentially the same situation understand and who can therefore be sympathetic to those explorations without being condescending.[42] Viewed from the perspective of the life cycle, the close friendships of adolescence contribute to personality stability and social growth. Weinberg found that during adolescence the closer friend was more important or equal to the mother as the closest confidante.[43]

As in childhood, the adolescent frequently experiences loneliness. And because that is a relatively new experience, and occurs at a time when relationships with others are highly valued, it can be very painful. For some persons, adolescence becomes the time when no one can provide the comfort and security associated with personal attachment. Parents may not be able to serve, and new friends do not emerge. As a result, the adolescent can experience all the symptoms of separation distress which is loneliness. There is some evidence that loneliness in adolescence forces persons into friendships, which is viewed as a release from loneliness. While children seldom express this function of friendship beginning with adolescence and extending through adulthood, a substantial minority speak of friends providing comfort simply by their company.[44]

For the adolescent to choose a friend as an escape from loneliness, or for any other reason, is not always a choice available to them. A number of adolescents remain friendless for periods. One study of junior and senior high school students found a relatively large number who were not selected as friends at any given time, and that often friendships that did develop were not always stable and lasting.[45] It may be that at any given time roughly 20 percent of all adolescents have no friends, and the percentage for adults may be even higher.

Weiss points out that during adolescence individuals become able to experience loneliness as well as separation distress. This capacity remains with them for the rest of their lives. A feeling of loneliness is often associated with the ending of a close relationship. The ending of a love affair, for example, may first produce separation distress and then, as the other is relinquished as an object of attachment, loneliness.[46] The loneliness is related to what is no longer there on the interpersonal level.

During adolescence popularity and friendliness become intertwined. To be popular means the individual has to be friendly. But friendliness usually stands for a pleasant recognition of the other and a positive response, not necessarily a deep involvement. It means that one includes the other into a wide grouping of people one is friendly with. But friendliness does not have the exclusiveness friendship had. Adolescents quickly learn that the closer and more intimate the friendship, the fewer the number of friends. They easily recognize the difference between being friendly with people and having friendships with a few individuals.

Increasingly, in the United States leisure time is spent away from home. And while this is true for all ages, it is especially characteristic of adolescents. For the adolescent something is not worth doing unless it can be done away from home. This is undoubtedly a reflection of the need for independence characteristic of adolescents. There is some evidence that leisure time spent away from home is more typical of boys than of girls, but it is increasingly becoming true for both sexes. One study found that in examining leisure, change and excitement were sought by the young while order and stability were sought by their parents. "Entertainment and variety are major interests of youth versus corresponding interests of performance and evaluation of parents."[47]

One of the major differences in friendships by sex, as will be examined in later chapters, is the greater incidence of revealing information in female friendships than in those among males. This pattern is already clearly established in adolescence. One study reported more girls disclosing more to their same-sex friends than boys. That study suggested that the tendency for girls to be more intimate with their friends may have been due, at least in part, to different reinforcements of intimate behavior. Where hand-holding and other signs of affection are acceptable between girls, such signs of intimacy are taboo among boys. "Since intimate behavior is rewarding for girls, it is likely that they will want to preserve the opportunity for continued intimate conversation by excluding others from their dyadic friendships."[48]

The taboos against males showing emotional feelings toward each other are already strong during adolescence. Many adolescent boys are uncertain about their new masculine roles and are therefore sensitive to any behavior that might threaten that role. The adolescent boy may become "super-macho" because he is unsure of himself in his new role. Often the boy learns that to be affectionate, gentle, and compassionate toward others is not to be "one of the boys." Inexpressiveness becomes a characteristic of many boys; it is based on a life-long institutionally based socialization process that starts with infancy. The male child learns that expressing emotions is not part of the male role.[49]

There are other differences in learning new social roles for girls and boys during adolescence. It may be that because of earlier physical development and convention society functions to encourage a shift from the role identity of child-to-female earlier than it does for the shift from child-to-male. "Thus it would appear that validating a self conception of 'femaleness' in much of our society requires affiliation with and feedback from others at an earlier age for females than for males."[50]

One study reports that the friendships of girls were of greater importance than were any opposite-sex friendships during the entire adolescent period. Furthermore, they were characterized by a maturity not observed in boy-to-boy friendships. "While the boy uses his friends within the peer groups to break away from his family and establish independence from the home, the girl looks to her 'best friend' as someone with whom she can talk and clarify her identity, especially her sexual self."[51]

A national survey of girls between the ages of 11 and 18 found that same-sex friendships tended to undergo regular changes from the early years through the later years of adolescence. Between the ages of 11 and 13 the girls formed friendships on the basis of mutually enjoyable activities. During that time the personal qualities of the friends were relatively unimportant and were described in superficial terms. The girls were mainly enthusiastic partners for various activities with their friends. But during middle and late adolescent years this picture greatly changed. The friendships came to be characterized by a sharing of experiences, emotional responsiveness, and intimacy. "There was much emphasis in the personal qualities of a friend, such as loyalty, the ability to keep confidences secret and give emotional support."[52]

Social class may also have a more important influence on the friendship of girls than boys. One study found that girls pay more attention to social class in the selection of friends than do boys. This same study also found that, in general, girls' friendships during the adolescent years are more fervent and reciprocal than are those of boys. In the 14- to 16-year age range girls frequently desire strong loyalty and absolute security in their same-sex friendships. They often express a strong need to be similar. "Girls tend to be more advanced than boys in interpersonal development during adolescent years judging from their more mature conceptions of friendship and greater ability to articulate them."[53]

Adolescence strongly features the emergence of cross-sex romantic relationships. This can often confuse the question of whether or not there can be nonromantic opposite-sex friendships. One study asked: "In your opinion is true friendship between boys and girls possible?" Three-fourths answered "yes." With age, however, doubts in this regard increase so that more than half of the male university students studied answered negatively.[54] Often an opposite-sex friendship will end when the person becomes involved romantically with another person because of suspicion directed at the opposite-sex friend. If one believes it must hold some romantic or sexual dimension, it is seen as threatening to the romantic relationship and often is forced to end.

One study of adolescents found that they generally believed that friendship does not cut across sex lines; this was true for both sexes. They believed that if it did, it became transformed, and the main transformation was a romantic one. This same study found the belief that a girlfriend or boyfriend was really not a friend.[55] This was because the emotions of friendship are seen as very different from those of romance and love. One common quality of romance is to further restrict the relationships of the individuals. Romantic involvement often means not only a high orientation to the love object but also that the partners increasingly isolate themselves from all others. An increase in a girl- or boyfriend's influence is accompanied by a lessening of other influences.[56] As a result, romance can be quite destructive to friendship with others.

With the development of romantic involvement, and its demands for heavy involvement, there is often no time for or interest in others. It may be that for many the period of high romantic involvement is the period of least friendship participation during their life cycle. To the extent that romance dominates their lives, there is no room for other relationships. This situation is described by a 21-year-old male:

> I remember when I fell in love with my girlfriend. We wanted to be together as much as possible. This left no time for friends, parents, or anyone else. It was like we were in a very small but intense world of our own. It was completely private to us and we didn't want to share any of it with others. When we went out we didn't want to see friends because there was so much to say to each other that we didn't want to be distracted by others.

NOTES

1. Rubin, Zick, *Children's Friendships* (Cambridge, MA: Harvard University Press, 1980), p. 18.

2. Ibid., p. 93.

3. DuBois, Cora, "The Gratuitous Act: An Introduction to the Comparative Study of Friendship Patterns," in E. Leyton, ed. *The Compact: Selected Dimensions of Friendship,* (Canada: University of Newfoundland Press, 1974), p. 23.

4. Rubin, *Children's Friendships,* p. 25.

5. Ibid, pp. 2-3.

6. Reisman, John M., *Anatomy of Friendship* (New York: Irvington Publishers, 1979), p. 114.

7. Selman, Robert L. and Anne P. Selman, "Children's Ideas About Friendship: A New Theory," *Psychology Today,* October 1979, p. 71.

8. Reisman, *Anatomy of Friendship,* p. 101.

9. Ibid., p. 73.

10. Rubin, p. 102.

11. Reisman, p. 116.

12. Rubin, p. 38.

13. Ibid., p. 39.

14. Reisman, p. 118.

15. Rubin, p. 96.

16. Bensman, Joseph and Robert Lilienfeld, *Between Public and Private* (New York: Free Press, 1979), p. 138.

17. Rubin., p. 69.

18. Holmes, Donald J., *Psychotherapy* (Boston: Little, Brown, 1972), p. 361.

19. Rubin, p. 10.

20. Reisman, p. 106.

21. Ibid., p. 106.

22. Rubin, p. 11.

23. Selman and Selman, "Children's Ideas About Friendship," p. 72.

24. Rubin, pp. 69-70.

25. Brenton, Myron, *Friendship* (New York: Stein and Day, 1975), pp. 66-67.

26. Eder, Donna and Maureen T. Hallinan, "Sex Differences in Children's Friendships," *American Sociological Review,* April 1978, p. 247.

27. Ibid., p. 238.

28. Rubin, p. 108.

29. Sommer, Barbara Baker, *Puberty and Adolescence* (New York: Oxford University Press, 1978), p. 121.

30. Kon, Igor S. and Vladimir A. Losenkov, "Friendship in Adolescence: Values and Behavior," *Journal of Marriage and the Family,* February 1975, p. 813.

31. DuBois, "The Gratuitous Act," p. 24.

32. Shulman, Norman, "Life-Cycle Variation in Patterns of Close Relationships," *Journal of Marriage and the Family,* November 1975, p. 813.

33. Brittain, Clay V., "Adolescence Choices and Parent-Peer Cross-Pressures," *American Sociological Review,* 28: 389 (1963).

34. Pleck, Joseph H., "Man to Man: Is Brotherhood Possible?" in *Old Family/New Family: Interpersonal Relationships,* N. Glazer-Malbin, ed. (New York: D. Van Nostrand Co., 1975), p. 236.

35. Floyd, H. Hugh, Jr. and Donald R. South, "Dilemma of Youth: The Choice of Parents or Peers as a Frame of Reference for Behavior," *Journal of Marriage and the Family,* November 1972, p. 632.

36. Sommer, *Puberty and Adolescence,* p. 12.

37. Selman and Selman, p. 71.

38. Kon and Losenkov, "Friendship in Adolescence," pp. 150-51.

39. Van Dine, E. Virginia, "Personality Traits and Friendship Formation in Adolescent Girls," *Journal of Social Psychology,* 17: 302 (1940).

40. Campbell, Ernest Q. and C. Norman Alexander, "Structural Effects and Interpersonal Relationships," *American Journal of Sociology,* November 1965, p. 286.

41. Weinberg, S. Kirson, "Primary Group Theory and Closest Friendship of the Same Sex," in T. Shibutani, ed. *Human Nature and Collective Behavior,* (Englewood Cliffs, NJ: Prentice-Hall, 1970), p. 309.

42. Bensman and Lilienfeld *Between Public and Private,* p. 139.

43. Weinberg, "Primary Group Therapy," p. 318.

44. Reisman, p. 108.

45. Horrocks, John E., and Murray Benimoff, "Stability of Adolescents' Dominance Status Over a One Year Period as a Friend by Their Peers," *Adolescence,* Fall 1966, p. 229.

46. Weiss, Robert S., *Marital Separation* (New York: Basic Books, 1975), p. 43.

47. Gunter, B. G. and Harvey A. Moore, "Youth, Leisure and Post-Industrial Society: Implications for the Family," *The Family Coordinator,* April 1975, p. 203.

48. Eder and Hallinan, "Sex Differences in Children's Friendships," p. 238.

49. Balswick, Jack, "The Inexpressive Male: Functional Conflict and Role Theory as Contrasting Explanations," *The Family Coordinator,* July 1979, p. 333.

50. Floyd and South, "Dilemma of Youth," p. 633.

51. Richmond-Abbott, Marie, *The American Woman* (New York: Holt, Rinehart & Winston, 1979), p. 151.

52. Ibid., pp. 150-51.

53. Sommer, p. 121.

54. Kon and Losenkov, p. 150.

55. Naegele, Kasper D., "Friendship and Acquaintances: An Exploration of Some Social Distinctions," *Harvard Educational Review,* 28(3): 245.

56. Otto, Luther B., "Girl Friends as Significant Others: Their Influences on Young Men's Career Aspirations and Achievements," *Sociometry,* September 1977, p. 287.

3

WOMEN AND FRIENDSHIP

When we look at friendship in society we can see many variations. But there is no social factor more important than that of sex in leading to friendship variations. As we have earlier discussed, when children grow up they very quickly enter into somewhat different socialization experiences depending on whether they are a girl or a boy. This leads to variations in the functions of friendship for the two sexes as well as how they perform as friends.

An examination of American history shows that when friendship has been recognized it has almost always been as male friendship. But there is now strong evidence as to the historical importance of friendship for women. A study by historian Smith-Rosenberg is based on the examination of correspondence and diaries of American women and men from 35 families between the 1760s and the 1880s. She shows the importance of female friendship for women during those years. Between many of the women there was a strong sense of love and emotional attachment. At that historical period such love was socially acceptable as well as compatible with values about marriage. During that period, as with most of American history, there was strong segregation of women and men.

Contacts between men and women were frequently formal and stiff. The world was divided between the world "out there" for the men and the world at home for the women. In the world out there the man functioned in a world of commerce, and his status was given by other men for what he attained in that world. While his family roles were seen as necessary and appropriate, they were usually not relevant to who he was. Not only was his world out there inappropriate for the woman, but he often saw himself as protecting her from its influences—influences inappropriate and improper for good women.

The world of the past was dominated by the double-standard when it came to many rights for women and men. This was often attributed to a biological cause—"that's the way women and men are," the belief was that men could best cope with the harsh realities of the world and women with the soft, emotional needs of the home and family. This double standard was reflected strongly in values about sexuality. As a result, prostitution was common because it could meet the "driving, uncontrollable sexual needs of men." The male could often further rationalize this by sanctimoniously believing he was protecting his wife from his sex crives, thereby maintaining her purity.

While in many ways women were isolated, their lives did have a basic integrity and dignity that came about through shared experiences and feelings for one another. What was important to that world was that women provided each other with mutual support. Criticism was discouraged, thus allowing a milieu where women could develop a sense of inner security and self-esteem. The outside, male-dominated world provided little such security. The basic relationship in the world of women was that of mother and daughter. As young girls grew older, their social growth was further developed through their relationships with their peers. Many upper-middle-class girls entered schools, where friendships flourished. "Young girls helped each other overcome homesickness and endure their crises of adolescence. Older girls in boarding schools 'adopted' young ones, who called them 'mother' ".[1]

Smith-Rosenberg found in the letters and diaries of teenage girls that boys were viewed as distant and unsually to be warded off. She suggests this was the result of the girls' sense of bonding as well as a kind of whimsey; the girls joked among themselves about the faults of boys. Rarely did they appear to exchange favorable comments about boys. While hostility and criticism of each other was rare–it seemed almost taboo–the young women allowed themselves to express a great deal of hostility toward peer-group men.[2]

As girls got older they sought marriage. But after marriage the worlds of women and men continued to be highly segregated. The men continued to often appear as an outgroup to the women. They were segregated into different schools, supported by their own male network of friends and kin, socialized to different behaviors, and coached to proper formality in courtship behavior. This meant that relationships between young women and men usually lacked the spontaneity and emotional intimacy that was common to the young women's ties with one another.

In general, Smith-Rosenberg found that the materials she examined supported the importance of emotional ties formed between women. Those deeply felt, same-sex friendships of women were casually accepted in American society. From at least the late eighteenth century through the mid-nineteenth century, a female world varied, and yet with structured relationships it seems to have been an essential part of American society. Those relations ranged from the "supportive love of sisters, through the enthusiasms of adolescent girls, to sensual avowals of love by mature women. It was a world in which men made but a shadowy appearance."[3]

Today it continues to be more socially acceptable for women to be emotionally and physically expressive to one another than is true for men. But in the past the level of physical and emotional expression between women was probably greater. This does not appear to have been an overtly sexual relationship; rather, it was based on emotional needs and close relationships not typically found among men. And much of the close interpersonal relationships between women did not have the sexual connotation it has today.

When we look into the past about friendships between women, it can be seen that many stereotypes and folk notions have been handed down. But there are no myths about devoted women friends that are comparable to those of Achilles and Patroclus or Roland and Oliver. Even Sappho and her friends have been relagated historically to the limbo of lesbianism on the shaky grounds of a few lines of verse.[4]

The "traditional wisdom" about female friendships has been to see them as inferior to those of men. This undoubtedly has been a reflection of a more general notion of female inferiority. If women are seen as inferior, then obviously what they do in most areas, including friendship, by definition will be inferior. Both women and men have often accepted this belief and downplayed women's friendships. With few exceptions, the models held forth in society of friendship have been about men and for men. As a result, women have often joined men in labelling women's friendships as amusing or trivial.

One review of historical and anthropological literature found that writers either failed to observe female friendships at all or treated them as a peripheral part of the social system. They were given importance only insofar as they supported the functioning of other parts of the social system. In general, significant female friendships have been ignored, interpreted as lesbian, or, when recognized, depreciated in importance. One consequence of this has been that for many women the ideology that women cannot trust each other or work together reinforces women's dependence on men.[5] Women have not particularly valued other women's friendships because they have accepted the belief that women are of less value than men.

Anthropologist DuBois writes that it is noteworthy how consistently all types of friendship, but especially best or close friends, are found to be both empirically and normatively more significant for men than for women. "In both Chinese society and in Mexican middle-class society, for example, women are not meant to have friends; they have kin and neighbours."[6] It has been traditionally assumed that women can have their needs for close interpersonal relationships satisfied through their family and kin relationships. In many societies men have friends and women have relatives.

In general, the more traditional the kinship values, the more hostile they will be to friendship. Kinship has long been believed to meet all the needs of the woman and the woman has been expected to find through her relatives the kinds of emotional relationships often associated with friendships. It has often been the case that friendship was seen to subvert kinship and by its very existence to threaten the values of kinship. This has been especially true with regard to women: they were often assumed to have a greater commitment to the family and to have their needs satisfied in those relationships.

One of the arguments against the real worth of female friendship has been made by de Beauvoir. She asserts that those friendships that women are able to maintain are important to them but are different from those found among men. She says that men communicate through ideas and projects of personal interest, while women are much more limited by their nature. "Women do not discuss opinions and general ideas, but exchange confidences and recipes, they are in league to create a kind of counter-universe, the values of which will out weigh masculine values."[7] If women in social gatherings talk about the trivia of fashion or cooking, the men are talking about automobiles and sports, hardly profoundly different topics.

Many women, even today, find that their adult status or prestige depends on their attachment to a male. And many women are willing to give up female friends, if necessary, in order to win the man. It can therefore be argued that when women are role-oriented in a traditional direction, friendships with other women will often become secondary. One study found that women were not loyal to each other when separated. But this is hardly surprising, for women gain little by remaining true to those who hold no power, especially if such loyalty threatens their attachment to those who really hold power—the men. For many role-oriented women competition for men is primary and friendship with other women secondary. As a result, many women will cut themselves off from meaningful relationships with other women. "Instead they were willing to maintain sexual relationships with men whose power and status they think will increase their own."[8]

Men interact with others in terms of roles. Because men tend to be outward-oriented, they construct roles to fit behavior. Men often see persons not as complete human beings but as persons filling particular roles. They may see another man as a lawyer, a competitor in tennis, a co-worker, or a drinking partner. In this sense, many men do not see women as full human beings. They rather turn to their sets of role expectations and assign to a woman a label the light according to in which they see her. They may choose whatever role seems most appropriate under the circumstances and offer responses accordingly. But women more often see the total person. This is reflected in the fact that women have fewer segmented, or specialized, friendships than do men.

I would argue that the historical beliefs in the inferiority of female friendships are wrong. The evidence clearly indicates that the friendships of women are more frequent, more significant, and more interpersonally involved than those commonly found among men. The friendships of women are more often based on trust and involve more revealing of the self to the other. The close relationships among women are generally defined as self-revealing and accepting, whereas the close relationships between men are subjectively defined in terms of doing things together.

Women more typically come from within themselves in their friendships with other women, while men typically function from outside themselves. The woman reveals her feelings, emotions, and insecurities. Often the man guards against letting out anything that reveals his feelings, especially if he sees them as threatening to his sense of masculinity. Men more often share by doing things together and showing enthusiasm for their shared activities, but they reveal little about what is going on inside them.

One factor that is crucial to the friendships of many women is the willingness to share. There is often a strength that can be gained by individuals based on having shared important feelings, thoughts, and experiences. Friends who have gone through a traumatic or happy experience may return to it in their later interactions. Those recollections can often strengthen their ongoing friendship. Sharing with friends stresses the highly positive and rewarding dimension of friendship.

Given the social structure of American society, women can usually form friendships easier than men. There is less accessibility of same-sex friendships to men once they pass early adulthood. Often friendship with many of the men they meet is difficult because those men are in the same work world and are in competition with them or are in positions of greater or lesser power. Neither setting is conducive to developing close friendships. Women more often than men actively seek out other people as potential friends. And because women are more willing to reveal parts of themselves, they set up a situation where the intimacy of friendship can develop. Women are generally more socialized to the skills of social interaction and are more relaxed and capable in new settings dealing with a few people.

The structure of the family during the early and middle child-rearing years provides women with more chances for friendship. Self-revealing interaction with a few close friends is often chosen by women in place of the types of social group activities common among men. Looking after a child and close friendships can often be shared in terms of time. Women can get together and do both with relative ease, whereas group activities often mean they have to make arrangements for child care. These close friendships with shared social activities are often the choice of younger women with children.

The period of time when women have young, dependent children may be a time when friendship is as important as at any time in their lives. The woman is often locked into the community and her only available possible friends are women like herself. Therefore they can provide each other with support and a sense of significance at a stage in life when the mother role is so dominant and they have few other options.

The evidence clearly indicates that female patterns of friendship are much more revealing and intimate than those found among men. This also appears to be true for older women. A study of elderly persons found that more women than men have intimate friendships and that sex differences persisted regardless of variations in age, marital or occupational status, or educational or socioeconomic level. The study found that generally the wife was the man's only confidante, whereas the woman's closest confidante was most likely to be a woman friend. This suggests that older men satisfy their needs for intimacy largely within the marriage, but women seek their gratification for such needs with their own sex. If this is the case, then the prevailing assumption that women "need" marriage more than men because they are more emotionally dependent may very well be wrong.[9]

Same-sex friendships clearly offer some important gains. Friendship and intimacy with members of the same sex can be important and valuable. For example, individuals of the same sex often tend to "see through" any phoniness or pretensions by another member of the same sex. The opposite sex is more easily fooled. It also appears that a person secure in her or his sexual identity feels comfortable with members of the same sex and is generally liked by them. One writer says that what can be gained by women in their friendships with each other is a close and meaningful intimacy. They can share ideas, share the secret corners of the self, trusting another with worries, joys, dreams and fears, express feelings, become vulnerable.[10] They can reveal with a high sense of security.

A 42-year-old divorced woman said:

> I love my women friends for their warmth and compassion. I can share anything about my life with them and they never pass judgment or condemn. They are very open and share much of their inner thoughts with me. These friends have helped me tremendously in my own personal growth and through great changes in my life. They are fun to be with and have a grand sense of humor. I would tell those women anything. There are no limitations on disclosure that I am aware of. The special quality of these female friendships is the openness. I have never been able to talk and share my feelings and experiences in the same way with any man.

In my study I found that a majority of the women believed there were some unique experiences of being female that contributed to the special nature of friendship with other women. A 40-year-old businesswoman said:

> Womanness does matter because of the same socialization. All of us have experienced being crapped on. But I don't think it is any sort of basic femaleness. But I certainly have become aware of women as sisters. Sisters in the sense of so many common experiences. I have also come to really feel good about my women friends.

The women were asked how many close women friends they had. The average number given was 4.7 friends. The average number given by the male respondents was 3.2 friends. For most of the women, having a number of friends was very important. There has been some argument that close friendships must be limited in number because the more friends one has the less close relationships tend to become. This would appear to be true at times, but the close friends of many of the women I interviewed were seen as close even though there may have been four or five. For many women, this may occur because there is a desire and an ability to devote a good deal of time and intensity of involvement with friends. If this is the case, it would seem likely that many women are capable of having several very close friends at the same time. The friendships among women, more so than with men, are less segmented. That is, the women give a full commitment and broad coverage to many of their female friendships.

Women who have a variety of friends tend overwhelmingly to form dyadic relationships—that is, in pairs, not in three- or more person groups. I found only one instance of a woman describing a friendship that was equal for all three people in it. This is in contrast to many of the friendships of men, which do include three or more persons. For women, the limiting of each friendship to two persons is often a reflection of the intensity of involvement. In general, the more we will reveal or commit ourselves interpersonally, the fewer the people with whom we are willing to enter into that kind of relationship.

The women were asked if they would and did reveal anything to at least one of their close friends. Sixty percent of the women said they did, in comparison with 35 percent of the men. A 45-year-old attorney said:

> I have four close women friends. I can be completely honest and self-revealing because they know everything about me. I can talk about all kinds of personal things. I think that friendships are more important than marriage. To have no friends would be worse than to have no marriage.

A 25-year-old graduate student said: "We have total acceptance of each other—we don't have to prove anything. I share and they accept and don't make value judgments about me. We can tell each other anything and that is why we are best friends."

I found after probing that some women who say they would reveal anything to a best friend often do not completely do so. This appears to happen because while we may give a great deal in friendship, we often draw a line around a part of ourselves. It may be difficult to reveal everything and still maintain a sense of privacy or integrity. Probably for most of us there is an important need sometimes *not* to share, to keep something of ourselves that is private and special. It is not that we don't trust our friends, but rather that what we hold we see as having significance only for ourselves. We may also not reveal something to friends to protect them from hurt or worry. A 32-year-old student said:

> I reveal a lot but not everything. I think everyone has an essential private core. There are some feelings about myself and others I won't reveal. I hesitate to share any negative feelings with my close friends. I think you should be careful in how much you unload on a good friend.

Women not only have more close friends than do men, but they are also more revealing. Jourard found that women also disclosed more information about themselves to the important people in their lives than did men. There was also a correlation between a friend was willing to disclose to the other and what the other disclosed to the friend–reciprocity in self-disclosure." Often as a friendship develops there is a kind of dance of moving forward in turns. Rapid revealing often ends many relationships before they can develop into friendships. We may feel the other person is saying too much or they are pushing us to reveal before we are ready to do so.

Booth found that female friendships were richer in spontaneity and confidences than males. He found that although spontaneity and affect seemed to characterize the close ties of the middle-aged, married, and white-collar respondents more than it did the elderly, unmarried, and blue-collar respondents, the sex differences in spontaneity and confiding behavior clearly showed in all categories. In those cases where the man was more spontaneous than the woman it seemed to be due to his early socialization experience. He had been reared with values conducive to spontaneity and confidante relationships. Booth found little evidence to suggest any that sociobiological aggressiveness among men leads to greater success in friendship.[12] If anything, aggressiveness is a limiting factor in friendship development.

I asked women what made for good friendships. The most common answers were shared experiences, interests, and values. Friends were also those with whom one could relax, receive support from, and share things with. They also described the feelings they had for their best friends in terms of love, affection, warmth, and comfortableness.

We know that the capacity for intimacy varies greatly among individuals and quite likely varies over the life cycle of most people. Probably more often women than men are able to establish and maintain relationships with a high degree of intimacy. There are social qualities to intimacy, in that we are socialized to believe that different kinds of emotional relationships are desirable and often are even a measure of our "healthiness." This is clearly more often the direction of socialization for women than for men. One study found a close relationship between intimacy and a sense of having a special or unique relationship. This intimacy was important because once a certain level was reached the friends felt bound to each other, and that led to greater revelations and greater involvement.[13]

Intimacy and closeness between friends is also reflected in the values extended to friends and beliefs about friendships. To say that we have a friend is partly to say we are not alone and that we matter to at least one other significant individual. The basic pleasure given by the friend is the good feeling of being reaffirmed and reassured by another. Friendship carries with it other kinds of pleasures. There can be the pleasures of laughter, excitement, and emotional release. The dimension of laughter is important–it means we can trust the other and relax with them to the point of sharing the good and pleasurable sensations of life. For friends laughing is sharing and being exuberant and not being superior or patronizing. As Greeley writes, friendship is "a very serious business and that is why they have no choice but to be comedians."[14]

The rapid changes that have occurred in the lives of many women in recent years point to the increasing importance of female friends. One study found that the long-range trend was the central importance of supportive female networks in raising women's aspirations and encouraging their creativity. In voluntary religious and charitable endeavors, social settlements, and colleges, women have have helped each other overcome the conflict between individual aspirations and cultural forces of traditional conformity. Those experiences have also decreased the isolation that had been so debilitating to many women. It may be that it was the isolation rather than the patterns of socialization–or even the family demands–that most undermined women. Historically this isolation took many forms: loneliness on the frontier, the domestic isolation in agricultural communities, or the psychological alienation of the 1950s.

The 1950s was the period of the "feminine mystique." This was, as described by Betty Friedan, a time of malaise, of frustration. Many women had what they had been taught would give them happiness, but they were not happy. They felt frustrated and short-changed but didn't know why. In this period women's friendships were valued very low, because the belief was that the woman should devote herself completely to her family and her home, and friendships were seen as distracting from those functions. That was also the time when women's friendships were seen as frivolous and superficial. Many women developed negative images of themselves when they were together in small groups. Women in small groups were not seen as teammates or colleagues, but as the "girls" trooping off to have lunch in a tearoom. The image was often of women dressed up to impress one another having a terrible time splitting the check. For many women and men, these kinds of stereotypes about women's friendships still exist.

Given the isolated nature of the world of women in the past, women developed patterns of coping by helping each other. For example, when women experienced emotional distress in their relationships with their husbands, mothers, and other family members, they turned to their friends to express their feelings. Female friendships have many times served as social supports for difficult marriages. Often the close friend is the only shelter of rationality and support for women caught up in family comflict.

Friendships among women are often long-lasting and seen as a dimension leading to closer and stronger friendships. Simon found that one-third of the women she studied traced their friendships back to before they were married, and about three-quarters were formed during grade and high school.[15] A 48-year-old secretary said:

> My friendships are long-standing; they have stood the test of time. And time and insight have taught me to stand back and evaluate slowly. There is no immediate "like" and no one has the ability to manipulate me to "like." My liking matures slowly.

My interviews found that most women do not feel that a long period of time necessarily need elapse for a friendship to become close. There must be sufficient time or interaction for the intimacy and closeness to develop, but once that happens, the friendship of a couple of months may be seen as being as close as one that goes back over many years. It may be a part of the folklore of friendship that the old friendships are the best friendships. People often describe an old friendship and say that while they have had very little contact with that person over the years they still consider them to be a good friend. Often the definition of friendship continues because we have a strong sense of loyalty based on it going so far back into the past. The old friendship may be little more than a memory to be treasured.

With old friends we don't see often there is, when we do get together, the returning to the past. What we recall tends to be the good things, the pleasant things. We don't have to see each other a great deal to remain close friends. Many friendships endure under conditions of infrequent contact and of being separated in time and space. With some friends the time separation seems like nothing when we see each other. We can meet and pick up after an absence of several years as if we had parted only yesterday. It may also be that some friendships thrive with limited contact because if we saw a lot of each other we might find that what we now have in common is not enough to sustain a more extended relationship.

While I have been talking about friendship in general, it can, of course, take on different meanings in different settings. This is illustrated in a study of nonworking English women who were married to men in management jobs. The study points out that in asking the women about their three best "friends" the term had several different meanings. The authors found that those women who said they had no best friends may have meant that they felt genuinely isolated or they may have meant they were among many friends but three could not be identified as "best." Or their interpretation of the term may have been such that a relationship would have to be exceptionally close before it could be put in the category of "best friend."[16]

As mentioned earlier, it has sometimes been assumed that women did not need friendship because they had family relationships. As long as that belief prevailed, it contributed to the belief that female friendship was second class or less important than all kinds of kinship ties. This suggests that in recent years the friendship of women has had to go through a legitimizing process. Seiden and Bart have written that the need is not so much to establish friendships between women as to legitimize them so that women and men may take them seriously and recognize that women often make real sacrifices to maintain them. "Some women have always done so—but for many women, legitimization of the fundamental importance of female friendships has been lacking in twentieth century America."[17]

It is likely that friendship has come to be of greater significance for middle-aged and older women in recent years. For example, there has been a recent increase in the divorce rates among women in their 40s and early 50s. While the vast majority of men who divorce at those ages remarry, this is not true for women. The number of women not remarrying may be a reflection of the low number of available men for remarriage. But probably more important is the option not to remarry. There is some evidence that that option is strongly supported by friendship networks of women of similar age and marital status. The friends provide the means for a social and interpersonal life without a husband. It also seems clear that women are better able to adapt to not having a husband than is the man to not having a wife.

As the woman becomes older, her greater life expectancy means fewer and fewer men from which to choose either marriage or friendship. Increasingly large numbers of older women share the status of widow and have that in common to develop a friendship. The need for the older woman to develop friends is important because those who lack female friends sometimes succumb to mental health problems.

Social class is also related to differences in friendship patterns for women. One study found that higher-status women had more close friends than did lower-status women. It was also found that lower-status women met greater proportions of their friends in the neighborhood than did the higher-status women. By contrast, higher-status housewives first met a greater percentage of their close friends at clubs and organizations and through their husband's work and their children's school.[18] When contrasted with working-class women, those women in the middle class have a wider community from which to draw their friends.

Another study points out that in the working-class marriage the wife tends to maintain close ties with relatives and old girlfriends while the husband continues to associate mainly with his friends from before his marriage. For the women, social and psychological support came not from marriage partners but from same-sex friends and kin. The friendships of the working-class women are more localized and circumscribed than not only those of the middle-class woman but also those of her male counterparts in the working class.

In the next chapter I will look at friendship in the work setting for men. In general, men often do not establish close relationships with people they work with because they are in competition or are in relationships of differing power. Women in the work force seem better able to develop friendships with co-workers. But the vast majority of women in the work force are in positions where upward mobility is very limited, so there is less reason for competition with their co-workers.

A study of young women sales assistants in a London department store found that pairs of women developed friendships. Over the course of their work day they would spend time in friendly and sympathetic conversation. They would develop an interest in each other's activities both inside and outside the store. They were ready to help each other whenever an opportunity occurred. The women would refer to each other as "my friend" and others in the store would recognize them as friends.[19]

Another study examined the development of friendships among academic women in a large university department. Kaufman found that, generally, the women sought occupationally based friendships more often than did their male colleagues. Often the women found comfort in surrounding themselves by same-sex colleagues and thereby legitimating their status as professor. The work friendships appeared more common to the unmarried women. The unmarried female professors had larger, more integrated, and more homogeneous networks than did the married women. Given traditional values, the unmarried professional women may have been the most stigmatized. "They may not only be 'primary deviants' at birth, 'double' deviants' as professionals, but also 'triple deviants' for not marrying."[20]

Because most professional-level occupations have contained, and continue to contain, a small percentage of women, they constitute a distinct minority. Such women often draw together in friendships for mutual support and because they can understand their common problems. A 36-year-old assistant professor in a large university department said:

> While some of my women colleagues are bitches, I feel close to most of them. This is because we have gone through the same kinds of experiences and had many of the same problems. Most of us have had the disadvantage of a much later start in academic life than men. While I am in some competition with another woman in the department for promotion, we are the best of friends. We don't like the fact that one of us will probably get promoted before the other, but that's life in a work world designed by men.

In recent years the emergence of the women's movement has had effects on friendships among women. Seiden and Bart believe that among women in the movement there have developed special feelings about friendship. They point out that while people make friends in all types of social movements, the women's movement has had as part of its ideology the belief in sisterhood. They report in a pilot study of 20 women active in the women's movement the overwhelming majority reporting that they had always had warm and significant relationships with women. It was not that they first found those friendships through the movement; rather, that the movement supported them in *conceptualizing the value of friendships.* Before that female friends had often had a "pasttime" quality, being regarded outside the arena of major action–something you had until "the" relationship comes along. In the past, friendships with other women had a quality of "play," while friendships with men had a quality of "investment" in terms of marriage prospects.[21]

In my research I asked women about the importance of the women's movement to their female friendships. Very few said it had any direct influence. However, most did say they had always had close relationships with other women. A number of them also reported that the movement had helped make them more aware of the value and significance of their female friendships. For our respondents the women's movement had been supportive rather than causative in their friendships.

Sometimes questions about sexuality enter into close relationships among same-sex friends. This is far more often a worry among men than among women. Seiden and Bart suggest there is probably an erotic component in most close friendships, and it appears to be disturbing to many people and is denied or repressed. They point out that lesbians usually make a distinction between their female friendships and their love or sexual relationships. "As with heterosexual couples there are some lover or sexual relationships which are not based on either love or friendship. And, of course, most lesbians, like most women in general, have female friends who are not lovers."[22]

It clearly appears that many American women have had, and often valued highly, their relationships with other women. What is important is that women's pride, dignity, self-respect, and effectiveness as human beings are enhanced by recognizing this. And when this happens all people stand to gain—women and men alike. It can be argued that, at least in the American middle class, female friendship patterns have been, and continue to be, more a basic primary relationship for women. These may develop in place of other relationships or along with them. But whatever the case, they perform the highly important interpersonal function of helping individual women more successfully cope with the emotional issues of life.

NOTES

1. Smith-Rosenberg, Carroll, "The Female World of Love and Ritual: Relations Between Women in Nineteenth-Century America," *Signs,* Autumn 1975, p. 19.

2. Ibid., p. 20.

3. Ibid., pp. 1-2.

4. Brain, Robert, *Friends and Lovers* (New York: Basic Books, 1976), p. 47.

5. Seiden, Anne M. and Pauline B. Bart, "Women to Women: Is Sisterhood Powerful?" in *Old Family/New Family,* N. Glazer-Malbin, ed. (New York: D. Van Nostrand Co., 1975), p. 194.

6. DuBois, Cora, "The Gratuitous Act: An Introduction to the Comparative Study of Friendship Patterns," in *The Compact,* E. Leyton, ed. (Canada: University of Newfoundland Press, 1974), p. 27.

7. de Beauvoir, Simone, *The Second Sex* (New York: Bantam Books, 1961), p. 511.

8. Forisha, Barbara Lusk, *Sex Roles and Personal Awareness* (New Jersey: General Learning Press, 1978), p. 188.

9. Blau, Zena Smith, *Old Age in a Changing Society* (New York: Franklyn Watts, 1973), p. 73.

10. Glazer-Malbin, Nona, *Old Family/New Family* (New York: D. Van Nostrand Co., 1975), p. 28.

11. Jourard, Sidney M., *The Transparent Self* (New York: D.Van Nostrand Co., 1971), p. 13.

12. Booth, Alan, "Sex and Social Participation," *American Sociological Review,* April 1972, pp. 186-87.

13. Kurth, Suzanne B., "Friendships and Friendly Relations," in *Social Relationships,* G. McCall, ed. (Chicago: Aldine, 1970), p. 141.

14. Greeley, Andrew M., *The Friendship Game* (New York: Doubleday, 1971), p. 83.

15. Simon, Rita James, Gail Crotts, and Linda Mahan, "An Empirical Note About Married Women and Their Friends," *Social Forces,* June 1970, p. 524.

16. Pahl, J. M. and R. E. Pahl, *Managers and Their Wives* (Harmondsworth, England: Penguin, 1971), p. 150.

17. Seiden and Bart, "Women to Women," p. 208.

18. Williams, Robin M., "Friendship and Social Values in a Suburban Community: An Exploratory Study," *Pacific Sociological Review,* Spring 1959, p. 10.

19. Bradney, Pamela, "Quasi-Familial Relationships in Industry," *Human Relations,* August 1957, pp. 274-75.

20. Kaufman, Debra Renee, "Associational Ties in Academe: Some Male and Female Differences," *Sex Roles,* 4: 19 (1978).

21. Sieden and Bart, p. 193.

22. Ibid., p. 221.

4

MEN AND FRIENDSHIP

The great friendships recorded in history have been between men. In the past when friendships among men have been romanticized and eulogized, they have been friendships reflecting bravery, valor, and physical sacrifice in coming to the aid of another. In most societies males have been valued more highly than females, and males have written almost all history. But rarely have the recollections been to celebrate interpersonal relationships of feeling, understanding, and compassion of one male for another. This has been so because masculine values have made those kinds of feelings inappropriate and highly suspect—they were unmanly.

Anthropologists have argued that men have superior and more meaningful friendships than do women. This argument has been presented in recent years by an American anthropologist, Lionel Tiger. He insists there are certain forms of camaraderie and gregariousness among men that do not occur among women. He even goes so far as to argue that the difference is not accidental or the result of cultural learning. "It is a profound aspect of the human career which is as explicitly biological as the reproductive encounter."[1] He offers no convincing argument as to this biological explanation. In fact, all the evidence indicates clearly that friendship patterns are learned behavior for both men and women and that they vary among individuals and over time in any given society.

Tiger has also asserted that the phenomenon of initiation can be seen as a male analogue to courtship in the male-female bond. He writes, "if a young male wants to join a specific group, then he must be prepared to display his eagerness to win this membership by suffering an array of humiliations, discomforts, fears and other oppressions."[2] This description is hardly typical of the experiences of American males in growing up. Tiger also sees an aspect of male-bonding as antifemale. He says that patterns of friendship among males exclude females from joining the male patterns. "Therefore, the argument is that friendship directly reflects basic social needs and it is entirely correct to see it as a vital expression of the nature of Homo Sapiens."[3] This argument suggests that the basic biological bent of men is to reject women. And while some men do reject women, that is clearly learned behavior, since most men do not.

Clearly implied in Tiger's thesis is a notion of biologically based male superiority; the notion of bonding presented is seen as clearly superior to anything women have. But there is no evidence that male bonding is biologically transmitted, and any evidence that it is socially true is highly questionable. It is a pseudo-scientific argument which wants to argue that women are genetically programed differently from men in friendship possibilities. But as another anthropologist, Robert Brain, points out, "any complete account of a woman's life cycle, reveals instances of important emotional and institutionalized bonds between girls, women and old ladies."[4]

Booth found that female friendships were richer in spontaneity and confidences than males. Although spontaneity and affect seemed to characterize the close ties of the middle-aged, married, and white-collar respondents more than it did the elderly, unmarried, and blue-collar respondents, the sex differences in spontaneity and confiding behavior clearly showed in all categories. In those cases where the man was more spontaneous than the woman, it seemed to be due to his early socialization experience. He had been reared with values conducive to spontaneity and confidante relationships. Booth found little evidence to suggest any sociobiological aggressiveness that yields greater success in friendship.[5] If anything, aggressiveness is a limiting factor in friendship development.

In the United States masculinity evokes a stereotype based on a romanticized past. Masculinity may be the Marlboro man, the all-American athlete, or a state trooper. The values are physical strength and courage, allowing the man to protect the weaker members of society—women, children, and the elderly. The stereotypic "real man" is stoic and does not reveal his emotions or feelings. Masculinity is almost always seen as outward-oriented; the man reveals little or nothing about what is inside him. By contrast, the female role has traditionally been emotional, expressive, and dependent.

For many American men there has been a kind of cult of *machismo.* This is often manliness by distortion and exaggeration. Machismo is an attempt by men not to feel. And if they cannot stop themselves from feeling, they must stop themselves from showing feeling—to feel is to reveal weakness. The ultimate machismo is the super-cool stud who never shows anything. He typically has only one facial expression—boredom, disdain, and noncommital. For him manhood is to be seen and acted out, but not to be felt and emotionally expressed. If one can see beneath the surface, then his machismo mask has slipped. He must quickly replace the mask or his feelings will show.

The coolness of men reaches into many areas of their lives. This is often the case in the area of sex, where being in control means to be cool and know exactly what to do in lovemaking—to be a successful lover. The man must be cool and controlled enough to bring his partner to orgasm. But often the concern is not really with her sexual pleasure, but rather that her orgasm reaffirm his skill as a lover and therefore satisfy his masculine self-image.

The continuing strength of the masculinity cult is based on the fact that many men prefer a social world populated by other men, and that social expectations and structure provide many opportunities for all-male activities. Many men prefer to spend time with each other where they can plan and make decisions together as well as enjoy shared leisure time. The evidence is clear that most men spend much less time with women than with other men. While they turn to women as sexual partners, that may be for no more than a few minutes a week. Sometimes it is just long enough for the man to establish a sense of heterosexuality. For many men, women are good to sleep with but not to stay awake with.

Many of men's energies are directed toward one another rather than to any heterosexual pursuits. One forty-year-old businessman said,

> Maleness really does contribute greatly to my friendships. The uniqueness of being male, women just would not be the same. I find it difficult to get close to women.

A thirty-five-year-old schoolteacher said:

> There is a special quality to being friends with men and it wouldn't be the same with women. With my male friends there is something special—I don't know what but it isn't there with women.

Often men interact with others in terms of roles. Because men tend to be outward-oriented, they construct roles to fit behavior. Men often see persons not as complete human beings but as persons filling particular roles. They may see another man as a lawyer, a competitor in tennis, a co-worker, or a drinking partner. In this sense, many men do not see women as complete human beings, labelling them, instead, according to their female roles. Men choose whatever role seems most appropriate under the circumstances and offer responses accordingly.

The world of men, much more than that of women, tends to be in nonfamily groups. These are typically groups organized around a specific activity. Men tend to be more comfortable in seeing each other in groups rather than on a one-to-one basis. The group situation defuses any possible assumptions about the intensity of feeling between men, and in that sense there is safety in numbers. This makes personal communication more difficult, but it provides what is often sought most by men in friendship—a mutual reassurance of masculinity.[6]

As was discussed in Chapter 3, women form dyadic friendships. This is in contrast to many of the friendships of men, which often include three or more persons. For women, the limiting of each friendship to two persons is often a reflection of the intensity of involvement. And because men reveal less, they can expand the size of their friendship groups.

Often men get together in groups for various kinds of games, and the game is the reason for getting together. Although women also use games as a reason to socialize, the real interest may be in communication rather than the game itself. By contrast, for many years I played poker in an all-male group every week. The only acceptable conversation, other than that related to the playing of poker, was brief kidding or needling exchanges. Any attempt at serious conversation was quickly ended by several of the players saying, "We're here to play poker and not for goddamn conversation. Play cards."

A major value in the American masculine world is to do—to be active and get things done. To do means to perform outward, to move into the world outside oneself. The measure of masculinity comes to be what can be shown and what others can see. The training of males to be doers is often at the cost of emotions and feelings. Males are taught that their feelings are to be controlled, channelled, or repressed. Even things that are discussed among men are often treated as if they are "out there." The few subjects that may be personal tend to be shaped as abstract general questions.

American men have long been able to deal with the inanimate objects of the world more easily than with other human beings. Men grow up to build and shape things; the interpersonal worlds have never been valued by men. Traditionally, if there have been emotional needs to deal with, they have been left to women. Men find it difficult to face up to the fears and anxieties they are not supposed to have if they are really masculine. Even recognizing how they feel, they may be unable to do anything about it. They may have ben so effectively socialized that they cannot confide in others sharing the reality in question—the competitive and striving nature of masculinity will make it especially difficult to share family fears with family members or work worries with work mates. The risk of having such fears confirmed as well founded seems too great. The fact that men are trapped within themselves has come through in our interviews. Women overwhelmingly reveal many of their fears, anxieties, and insecurities to their best friends, while men overwhelmingly do not. The close friendship between women is generally defined as self-revealing and accepting, whereas the close friendship between men is subjectively defined in terms of doing things together.

The less personal and more superficial levels of communication among men have many implications. It is not only that men disclose less to others than do women, but that of all the disclosures that go on among people, women are the recipients of more disclosure than men. Jourard found that while men often have good intentions to promote happiness in others, they often "miss the target." "That is, they will want to make the other person happy, but their guesses about the actions requisite to the promotion of this goal will be inappropriate, and their actions will appear awkward and crude. The men, blocked by pride, dare not disclose their despair or need."[7]

Sometimes men try to overcome their difficulty in communicating with one another through joking relationships. Something emotionally important to them will be presented in a joking or kidding manner because they would not be able to deal with it in a serious and straightforward manner. Anthropologists have found that among men in many cultures a joking relationship allows for friendliness expressed through a language of hostility. Mutually abusive behavior is softened by joking, eliminating offense. For example, one man may call his friend "a cheap bastard" or tell him "you are the ugliest son-of-a-bitch I've ever seen." Not only is this not taken as an insult, but it may even be spoken and interpreted affectionately. These kinds of insulting exchanges appear to be quite rare among women.

As mentioned in the previous chapter, my study found that the average number of close friends for men was 3.2 as against 4.7 for the women. Among the men, 10 percent said they had no close friends, but this was not true of any of the women. Because men in our sample were highly educated, they probably had more friendships than did less educated men in general. It is likely that the average number of male friends would be less for the middle class; among this group some men may have no friends at all. Lewis found that many males have never in their adult lives had a close male friend. Many have not known what it means to love and care for a male friend without shadows of some guilt and fear of peer ridicule. "Because of these restrictive norms, even those who have made friends usually have experienced little trust, little personal sharing, and low emotional investments in these friendships."[8]

About one-third of the men in the present study said they would reveal everything to at least one best male friend. Over two-thirds of the men who would not fully reveal said there are some personal insecurities they would not tell about. A 38-year-old advertising executive said:

> I have three close friends I have known since we were boys and they live here in the city. There are some things I wouldn't tell them. For example, I wouldn't tell them much about my work because we have always been highly competitive. I certainly wouldn't tell them about my feelings of any uncertainties with life or various things I do. And I wouldn't talk about any problems I have with my wife or in fact

> anything about my marriage and sex life. But other than that I would tell them anything. [After a brief pause he laughed and said:] That doesn't leave a hell of a lot, does it?

Fasteau has observed that some men do not share even the ordinary uncertainties and half-formulated plans of daily life with their friends. And if they do they tend to carefully suggest that they already know how to proceed—that they are not really asking for help or understanding.[9] This is in contrast with women, who are much more willing to reveal as well as ask for help from another woman.

In studies of the interactional patterns of same sex groups, the men in all-male college groups were found to be much less intimate and open than were the women in all-female groups. "In fact, the men talked very little of themselves, their feelings, or their relationships with significant others, whereas the women frequently did."[10]

Among mixed groups it has been found that women usually make the first references about themselves to the others present. Then the men join in without having the onus of initiating a discussion of "personalities." Collectively, the men can "blame" the conversation on the women. "They can also feel in those conversations that since they are talking 'to' the women instead of 'to' the men, they can be excused for deviating from the masculine norm."[11]

There is also the myth that women are bigger gossips than men. There is likely to be as much gossiping among men as among women, but what differs is the content. Women more typically than men gossip about the appearance or behavior of another woman. They may talk about her bad taste in clothes or in a boyfriend. By contrast, men more typically gossip about the "inner" man. They may talk about another man being stupid, incompetent, or dishonest. Such criticism is generally meant to imply that the speaker possesses the opposite, and therefore better, qualities.

The taboos against significant revealing among men are based in several areas. Probably the most important is tied to masculinity insecurities which may be closely linked to fears about homosexuality. The male's acceptance of the traditional male role is tied to the fear about his masulinity in part because he often sees any emotional intimacy between himself and another man as being viewed as homosexual. One study found that homophobia, the fear of homosexuality, was more characteristic of people who were rural, white, first-born, reared in the Midwest and South, most religious, and most conforming. The personality correlates were more authoritarian, dogmatic, intolerant of ambiguity, status-conscious, sexually rigid, guilty and negative about their own sexual impulses, and less accepting of others in general.[12]

For many men, it appears to be difficult and embarrassing to tell one of their best friends that he is liked. One nationwide survey found that a majority of all the men questioned had never told their best male friend that they liked them. As mentioned, for many men to tell a friend he is liked is best done in a negative, joking way. When one man says to another, "you're not such a prick after all," or "you dumb son-of-a-bitch you're OK," they are really saying "I like you." Fasteau suggests that drinking provides many males with a setting in which they can be more revealing to their friends. In a drunken conference men can exchange confidences and periodically loosen the restraint against expressing a need for sympathy and support from other men—which may explain its importance as a male ritual.[13] Often what is revealed or displayed in a drunken exchange is not to be brought up when both friends are sober.

Fasteau goes on to suggest that when men do get personal in their talk with other men, it is often because their problems have gotten the best of them and they simply must talk to someone. And men that are not driven to despair do not talk about themselves, so "the idea that self-disclosure and expressiveness are associated with problems and weaknesses becomes a self-fulfilling prophecy."[14]

In recent years there has been an interest among some male social scientists in what they see as the "inexpressive male" in the United States. This type is described as a man who never shows any weaknesses, even with his friends and is therefore under the additional burden of keeping secrets about his weaknesses, his errors, and his pains. Many American men become so skillful at hiding their feelings and thoughts that not even their wives or closest friends know when they are depressed, anxious, or afraid.[15] Balswick suggests that probably most sexist behavior shown by American men is not self-consciously intentional. Rather, it is one of the functions of inexpressiveness—to keep males in positions of power in a sexist society.[16]

For many middle-class American men, it is the competitive world of work that is both the cause and the effect of many of their behavior patterns. In the competitive world the male typically believes he has to stay away from revealing much about himself. He often feels he has to keep his own counsel, and this often leads to isolation and loneliness. Some men feel their isolation is worth the rewards of their successes. A major problem for many men is acknowledging their fears and anxieties. However, even men who acknowledge such fears may be unable to do anything about them. They may have been so effectively socialized that they cannot confide in their wives or friends.

Often the measure of success in the competitive work world is a man's ability to control. In this setting competition is the principal means by which men relate to one another, in which they can demonstrate the masculine qualities of unwavering toughness and the ability to control. Often the result is that they may behave competitively in situations which do not call for it. For example, in conversations, often the man must show that he knows more about the subject than the other man.

In general, the greater the degree of competition, the less the affectional relationships. In competition many men get caught up in "power trips," the need to show power. Very often these power trips are directed toward other men as the means of winning approval, wealth, and prestige. It therefore becomes difficult for men to mutually disclose much about themselves because the disclosure can lead to increased vulnerability in the competitive setting. Typically men are primarily concerned with winning, while women are more often oriented toward achieving some equitable outcomes that will be as satisfying as possible to all concerned. Competition among men often becomes a barrier to intimacy between them. "Since a main form of winning is exploiting the opponent's weaknesses, men close themselves off from each other so they do not expose any vulnerabilities."[17]

There are a number of status differences that can make friendship difficult. In most instances friendship must be between equals, and where there are significant status differences friendship may be very difficult, if not impossible. In the work situation friendship between persons at different levels in the same hierarchy are often thought to compromise one's judgment because it balances a person's duties in the hierarchy against their personal inclinations or feelings. This is seen in the belief that a president of a company can have no close friendships with those who work for him. It might be possible for him to be friendly with someone in areas outside the work situation—for example, they might share an interest in sports—but he would have to prevent the friendship from intruding into the work relationship.

The attitudes a man holds toward his occupation have an important bearing on friendship patterns. In general, if a man does not value his work experiences, then friendships are less likely to arise in that setting. Probably people in social group settings they do not value highly are not attractive as potential friends.

For many men, the work situation so dominates their lives that it provides little time for them to develop friendships there. Friendships cannot flourish unless some time and interest can be invested. One study of managers found that many of them had little time and few interests other than their work. For those men involved in a sport, that common activity led to friendship away from the place of work. But what seemed to be valued was often the activity rather than the relationship.[18] If the sport is tennis, one does not want to give up the game if his partner loses interest. The man typically does not leave tennis to do something else with the friend, but rather finds a new friend with whom to play tennis.

A large part of the modern American work world today is bureaucratic, whether it be government, business, universities, or any large enterprise. Bureaucracies are based on total impersonality; the qualities of different individuals are not to influence decisions. Often bureaucracies fear that personal interaction may interfere with smooth operation and disturb the lines of communication and authority. Bureaucracies have traditionally tried to prevent the formation of cliques among the workers because these are seen as threatening to the bureaucratic order.

But there are some kinds of bureaucratic work situations in which friendships are seen at least partly as functional and therefore to be encouraged and controlled by the organization. A good example is found in some parts of the U.S. Army. A study of the social system of a army platoon found networks of interpersonal linkages. Everyone was a buddy, but one man usually more so than others. The buddy choices were private decisions and were not seen as threatening the solidarity of the squad or platoon. There were certain expectations among buddies. They were expected to "understand" in a deeply personal sense and so they became "therapists" to one another. The more one buddy told another, the more each depended on the other. Whatever they heard from each other they kept to themselves.

Although one man might think of another as a buddy, he seldom stated it publicly or boasted of the attachment. Buddies did not brag about individual combat skills or compare combat proficiency. In a crisis, and if forced to make a choice, a man would think first of his loyalty to a buddy, and second of his obligations to the organization.[19] While the military encouraged a buddy system during combat, it demanded that the partners return to the "normal life" when back at the base. This is because the buddy values are often seen as contradictory to the duties and roles of the army when in a noncombat situation.

There are differences between the friendships of middle-class men as compared to working-class men. In general, working-class men and women have less interpersonal involvements with both kin and friends than do the middle class. It also appears that working-class men reveal less about themselves to their friends than do middle-class men. Often their friendships are based in bars, clubs, and other social gathering spots for men only. There is a common tendency to carry friendships from their single days into their marriages, but these are typically maintained outside the home and have little to do with wives or other family members.

Among working-class men there is much less competition in the work situation than among men in the middle class. This is because there is very little chance for upward mobility in the working-class occupational world. The percentage of all friendships among working-class men based on their jobs is probably greater than is true for middle-class men. These friendships are often limited to work or time together after work–but not at each other's homes. Friendships on the job are typically not strong enough to hold a man to that job. No matter how friendly the work group to which he belongs, the worker is not likely to stay on the job just because of that group relationship. He often assumes that his next job will furnish him with just as good a group of men to work with. When less is expected in friendship, friends are more easily interchangeable. This appears to be more often a characteristic of working-class male friendships.

Sometimes in blue-collar occupations worker-friends direct some of their shared energies against the work. For example, in an automobile factory, work buddies may decide to undercut the set production rates or to commit job sabatage. The friends on the job are the main source of identification and not the job. The job may actually serve as a negative source and the workers will develop a shared antagonism toward work. Of course, management is well aware of this and will often attempt to reduce the chances that work friendship groups will develop or maintain themselves for very long.

Friendships among middle-class men may also be influenced greatly by their family involvements. One study found that families tended to be more home-centered in their leisure activities during the years when their children are young. At this stage men had their fewest friendships: the family so dominated the husband's activities and interests that it became the central institution around which all other activities were planned. Friends were friends of the family and leisure activities were family leisure activities.[20]

The above study found that when the children were teenagers, the measure of happiness shifted away from the family and correlated with fathers' jobs, health, and friends. "This stage seems to be a return to an outward looking perspective where the worlds of work and community are important sources of satisfaction."[21] It was further found that the frequency of agreement with the item, "I like a very active social life," declined as persons entered their 30s, recovered during their 40s, and then declined one more at about age 50. "When obligations to children loosen, it becomes more possible to seek happiness in nonroutine, extrafamilial events."[22] The men turn more to friendships at that time.

I found in my interviews that often friendships with men exist both away from the job and away from home. Partly because many male relationships are based on doing things together, they must do them away from home. To go bowling or hunting means to leave the home. Even when men want to drink together, they go to a bar more often than to one another's home. Sometimes men gather at one man's home to play cards, but typically when that happens the home is adapted to their needs: the family is kept away from them.

The masculine world, with its outward orientation, has perils for men. In competing they rely on each other as gauges of success or failure. But man not only measures himself against others; often as he gets older he measures himself against himself. He will often become disturbed that he can't do things as well as he once could. And man also fears how he will measure up in the future. Seifenberg observes that older men who believe they have not measured up or that their identify is incomplete or has suffered erosion are likely to view themselves and the world in most unkind ways.[23] I have found in interviews that while men may withhold very personal feelings from even best friends, the degree to which they reveal themselves to an interviewer indicates that they can and will reveal a good deal to a "suitable and safe other."

Many friendships come to an end. Probably the most common way for them to end is over time, with the two persons drifting apart and losing contact. But on other occasions the end of a friendship may be dramatic because of what one or both friends see as a break in the acceptable norms of friendship. For a friendship to end both parties must participate even though it may not be the desire of each. Friendships are not ended by others outside the relationship, although either partner may believe that "outsiders" can affect it. Others can contribute to or be the cause of a breakup, but only through their influence on one or both friends.

Sometimes a person may try to narrow or limit a friendship and find that the other continues to hold him to the old bargains. The second friend wants to continue what the first friend wants changed. This is similar to what happens in many romances, and, as in friendships, when there are significant differences in what is wanted from the relationship, strains increase and unhappiness and frustration result. An attempt may be made by the less committed friend to ease the strain by devaluing himself, or confessing the inability to hold up his end of the relationship, or trying to convince the other that someone else might make a better friend.

Because a great deal of emotional attachment is involved in friendships, we associate sadness with their loss. Friendships that end through death are especially severe losses. Thoreau wrote that "on the death of a friend, we would consider that the fates through confidence have devolved on us the task of a double living, that we henceforth to fulfill the promise of our friend's life also, in our own, to the world.[24] Relationships with either family members or friends are highly important to most of us, and we grieve their loss. The lost partner seems irreplaceable; no substitute could fill the emotional gap.

Because friendships involve such a high level of trust and confidence, ending them can be traumatic. A 53-year-old professor told about the dramatic end of a friendship:

> I had a best friend through my undergraduate days in college. The two of us were quite active in the radical student activities of that time. We did things together and we talked endlessly about the state of the world with what we thought was great profundity and insight. We had the answers and we both knew it because we thought alike. After several years of this friendship something happened that we violently disagreed about. This was a very major political event of the time when President Truman recalled General MacArthur from Korea because of his refusal to obey orders. I, as any radical would (in my mind), knew that Truman had no choice. But my friend argued that Truman was wrong. To me that point of view was so inconsistent with everything we believed in that not only was it intolerable but it was inconceivable. The argument actually led into the last fist fight I ever had in my life. And we never spoke to one another again.

To love, to trust, to confide, to reveal—all suggest vulnerability. When we feel those are battered and bruised, we feel grief and pain. Because women are more often emotionally involved in their friendships, they may find a loss of a friend through an emotional break even more upsetting than would men. A 36-year-old woman graduate student said:

> I was terribly upset when I found my best friend had told others some things I had told her in privacy. I was having trouble with my boyfriend and told her about it and it got back to me. I felt hurt but also that she had let me down. And as a friend I never dreamt she would do something like that. I guess we usually assume our friends are good friends and trustworthy and that's why it is such a shock when they are not.

The loss of a friend is also often a lonely experience. After a break with a friend or romantic partner we want support, but there really isn't any kind of support another person can give us. Often adjusting to the loss of a friend is like adjusting to bereavement—it takes time. With broken friendships, as with some broken romances, we often try to cope by making new friends. This is probably not too successful, because friendships "on the rebound" often mean we want to use the new person in some way, and using another person is inappropriate to the values of friendship.

When we look at friendship comparisons between men and women, what does the evidence show? It suggests important differences between men and women in the meaning of friendship and the extent to which it enters their lives. The basic difference is the stress on intimacy and revealing for female friendships and for sociability and coolness in the friendships of men. The evidence also suggests that women have more friends than do men. Both the nature and the extent of female friendship is gaining greater support in American society. There does not appear to be much change in the nature and acceptance of new levels of male friendship.

A shift for men would mean a move from the public to more private aspects of friendship. For men to enter more into private, intimate types of friendship would mean they would have to make important psychological and social commitments and changes. This would mean the development of new relational skills that would call for changes in men's views about competition, sexism and its values about male supremacy, and especially about fears of homosexuality. Such fears often involve far more than overt sexual behavior; they also include all "effeminate" qualities. These can include compassion, aesthetic interests and feelings, and the expression of such emotions as fear or personal hurt by crying or reaching out to another.

It may be that many males in American society want to become more expressive and open in their feelings. Many men have benefited from such expression, from the reduced potential for ulcers and other anxieties caused by pent-up emotions to freer and more intimate interpersonal relationships with family members and friends.[25] But to do so means giving up many of the value commitments to notions of traditional masculinity. And it is difficult to give up what has been a part of your life for so many years. The socialization to sex roles can be so powerful that for some men they are difficult, if not impossible, to overcome.

NOTES

1. Tiger, Lionel, "Sex-Specific Friendship," in *The Compact,* E. Leyton, ed. (Canada: University of Newfoundland Press, 1974), p. 44.
2. Ibid., p. 47.
3. Ibid., p. 48.
4. Brain, Robert, *Friends and Lovers* (New York: Basic Books, 1976), p. 48.
5. Booth, Alan, "Sex and Social Participation," *American Sociological Review,* April 1972, pp. 186-87.

6. Fasteau, Marc Feigen, *The Male Machine* (New York: Delta Books, 1975), p. 17.

7. Jourard, Sidney M., *The Transparent Self* (New York: D. Van Nostrand Co., 1971), p. 39.

8. Lewis, Robert A., "Emotional Intimacy Among Men," *Journal of Social Issues,* 34: 108 (1978).

9. Fasteau, *The Male Machine,* p. 13.

10. Lewis, "Emotional Intimacy Among Men," p. 116.

11. Fasteau, p. 10.

12. Lewis, p. 113.

13. Fasteau, p. 9.

14. Ibid., p. 11.

15. Lewis, pp. 113-14.

16. Balswick, Jack, "The Inexpressive Male: Functional Conflict and Role Theory as Contrasting Explanations," *The Family Coordinator,* July 1979, p. 334.

17. Lewis, p. 112.

18. Pahl, J. M. and R. E. Pahl, *Managers and Their Wives* (Harmondsworth, England: Penguin, 1971), p. 159.

19. Little, Roger W., "Buddy Relations and Combat Performance," in *The New Militancy,* M. Janowitz, ed. (New York: Russell Sage Foundation, 1972), p. 210.

20. Harry, Joseph, "Evolving Sources of Happiness for Men Over the Life Cycle: A Structural Analysis," *Journal of Marriage and the Family,* May 1976, p. 294.

21. Ibid., p. 293.

22. Ibid.

23. Seidenberg, Robert, *Marriage Between Equals* (New York: Anchor Press, 1973), pp. 77-78.

24. Shepard, Odell, ed., *The Heart of Thoreau's Journals* (New York: Dover, 1961), p. 11.

25. Balswick, "The Inexpressive Male," p. 334.

5

CROSS-SEX FRIENDSHIP

Over the years probably the most universal restriction on friendships has been to limit them to persons of the same sex. There are relatively few references in anthropology to socially approved close friendships between men and women that had no significant courtship or sexual implications. A few societies have minimized sex differences, and women in these societies were allowed considerable interpersonal freedom. There have been some instances where women were considered capable of having significant friendships and where cross-sex friendships were more often casual than close and were probably not exclusive.[1] In general, the view has been that women were less capable of developing friendships than were men.

The anthropological and historical data clearly indicate that sexually differentiated social behavior is nearly universal. In general, a cross-cultural comparison of data shows that males are more sexually active, more dominant, more deferred to, more aggressive, less responsible, less nurturant, and less expressive than females. In general, the social restrictions have centered on controls over possible sexuality. The possibility that females and males might want to be friends in nonsexual ways generally has not been considered enough of a social reality for social sanctions to have developed.

Smith-Rosenberg, in her study of friendship in nineteenth-century America, found that boys appeared distant and were warded off by girls. She wrote that while "hostility and criticism of other women were so rare as to seem almost taboo, young women permitted themselves to express a great deal of hostility toward peer-group men." She went on to say that it was not that the young women totally rejected the young men, because they did seek them for marriage. However, "the relations between young men and women frequently lacked the spontaneity and emotional intimacy that characterized the young girls' ties to each other."[2]

Historically, in American society the major restrictions against cross-sex friendship have centered on the belief that women were less capable of friendship than men. For example, philosopher George Santayana wrote that friendship with a woman was likely to be more or less than real friendship. It would be less because there was no intellectual equality or more because "there is something mysterious and oracular about the woman's mind which inspires instinctive deference and puts it out of the question to judge what she says by masculine standards."[3]

Over time variations have occurred in the social acceptance of cross-sex friendships. In the twentieth century the pattern has been to accept a high level of heterosexual interaction, but it has been restricted mainly to the young and the unmarried. While single people are allowed a great deal of latitude in developing relationships with the opposite sex, once they enter marriage that freedom is drastically restricted. Cross-sex relationships in American society have come to be both permissive and restrictive, depending on one's marital status.

The most important values that affect cross-sex friendships are those associated with marital status. In general, same sex and same marital status are seen as necessary for the development of friendships. One is not expected to seek out and develop a relationship with a person of another marital status, especially if they are of the opposite sex. The social norms of friendship stress similarities and relationships that support the institution of marriage: adults' cross-sex needs can and should be met only through marriage. In effect, marriage often means the exclusion of all others of the opposite sex as possible friends.

The possibility of sexual involvement is another factor that strongly influences the development of cross-sex friendships. Except during courtship, men and women are not expected to pursue interaction voluntarily with one another. And certainly not at any time should there be sexual component to that interaction. Even when they are unmarried, they are usually not encouraged to form friendships with one another, but to try to find a marriage partner. Thus the common belief is that men and women can be lovers but not friends. In part this is because being lovers places some social controls over sexuality, while being friends does not. The social expectation that cross-sex friendships will not be formed is also based on fears of exploitation in sexual relationships. Implied is that often the male develops the friendship as a means of sexual exploitation.

As was suggested in earlier chapters, the norms of friendship place a high value on similarity of social characteristics. Therefore, the members of most friendships tend to be of similar age, educational level, and so on. However, in cross-sex friendships there appears to be somewhat less homogeneity. Booth and Hess found that cross-sex dyads were less homogeneous than same-sex friendships. In cross-sex dyads males were found to be older and better educated than females. These features placed the males in a superordinate position relative to the women in the relationship. The men in the study tended to report younger female friends more often than they reported younger male friends. Similarly, the women reported older male friends more often than they reported older female friends. "Such preferences are consistent with prevailing norms pertaining to choice of sexual partners. Much less important to the male is his female friend's education. However, the female finds this an attractive attribute."[4] The Booth and Hess findings agree with the research on mate selection: the higher the education of the male, the greater his worth in the marriage market. In mate selection being older and having a better education are strongly favorable for men but unfavorable for women.

Let us look further at the available research information on the frequency of cross-sex friendships. In the Booth and Hess study the reported number of close friends of the opposite sex was not great. Thirty-five percent of the men and 24 percent of the women reported cross-sex friendships. Booth and Hess were mainly interested in the somewhat high rate of cross-sex friendships for men. They suggest that several factors may account for the differences. First, the norms that restrict cross-sex friendship development may have different effects on males and females. Second, women are more restricted than men. Third, there are different opportunities for men and women to meet members of the opposite sex. This is especially true of nonworking, married women, who have little chance to meet men.

Booth and Hess also suggest that men may feel less constrained in reporting cross-sex friends, while the woman may feel somewhat greater social taboos in naming a man as a good friend. They also found that women were more likely than men to limit the use of the title "close friend" to the people with whom they confide.[5] It has been found in other studies that men will more often use the term "friend" to describe a close relationship than will women.

In a study carried out among its readership, *Psychology Today* found that about three-fourths of the respondents felt that friendships with someone of the opposite sex were different from same-sex friendships. A major reason given for the difference was that sexual tensions complicated the relationship. The other reasons included having less in common with the opposite sex and the fact that society does not encourage such friendships.[6]

In my study of friendships, at the time of the interviews, 10 percent of the women said they had no close friendships with men and 34 percent of the men had no friendships with women. Of those who had friendships with the opposite sex, the average number for the women was 3.0 and for the men, 2.4. For both women and men, there appeared to be differences in friendships with same-sex in contrast to opposite-sex persons. In general, respondents said they would reveal more to a same-sex friend than to an opposite-sex friend. There were a variety of reasons for this. Some saw friendship as inappropriate with the opposite sex. A 30-year-old school teacher said:

> I have no close male friends because my husband won't allow it. In our relationships with couples if I talk to the man alone he really gets angry. He is jealous—both sexually and because I have interests with the other man that he is not a part of.

In general, both women and men say they feel closer to same-sex friends and would reveal more to them than to opposite-sex friends. A 40-year-old businesswoman said:

> With women I can share and relate because they, like me, have had children and faked orgasms. Men don't know how to be companions. They don't have the ability to just be they have got to have a purpose and be doing things. But basically with my women friends we all know where we are coming from—but with male friends there is always a part that is unknown.

Many of the men in our study reported that they placed strong restrictions on their friendships with women and on what they would reveal to them. In general, they would not reveal sexual matters, personal feelings, and sorrows or insecurities. One forty-year-old broker said:

> I avoid serious discussion with women because basically I see them as intellectually inferior. Besides they get too damn emotional if the discussion really gets going. I simply cannot relate freely to women. I can't sit down and drink with them and be myself like I can with my men friends. And there is always the fact that in being a man you don't want to let them see any weaknesses. If women see any weaknesses in you you lose manhood points in their eyes.

Another factor that differentiates women and men's cross-sex friendships is the opportunity to meet potential friends. Certainly the housewife who is restricted to the home and a social world of other women and children has few opportunities to meet men, and few opportunities for friendship to develop with any she does meet. The evidence clearly indicates that working women are more likely to have male friends than are nonworking women because working provides greater opportunities. A further limitation is that there are few social organizations that encourage cross-sex friendships. Most social organizations in the community are sexually exclusive or dominated by married couples. There are very few social organizations that encourage cross-sex friendships.

I found in a study I conducted in Australia that friendship between men and women, especially after marriage, had severe limitations. Even more so than in the United States, most Australian women are taught early in life that their world is to be for the most part separate from men. Males often do not admit women into friendship except under special circumstances and in a special capacity. Women see the male world as excluding them and therefore excluding possible friendships with men. Only 31 percent of the women studied said they had any close male friends. The women were asked to respond to the statement: "A married woman should be able to have private friendships with other men if she so desires." To this a little over half of all the respondents agreed. But the data also clearly showed that the higher the education of the woman, regardless of age, the more committed she was to the belief that she can have friendships with men and that the traditional taboos against cross-sex friendships should be broken down.[7] These findings are similar to those in American studies. The higher the education of the woman, the greater the resistance to sex segregation in many areas, including friendship.

As was suggested, there are a variety of barriers against cross-sex friendships. Along with sexual taboos there are a number of psychological and social constraints. Maslow found that some males develop psychological response sets for rejecting at least certain types of women. For example, "most males are not sexually drawn to strong, assertive, self confident females. Psychologically strong and mature males can be drawn."[8] Maslow believes many men are afraid of women because they see the women as reflecting their own "femaleness," softness, tenderness, and so on, which are qualities men do not want to see in themselves. He found that only as men become stronger and more self-integrated can they tolerate and enjoy self-actualized women, women who are full human beings. For Maslow strong men and strong women are the condition of each other, and neither can exist without the other. "They are also the cause of the other because women grow men and men grow women. And finally of course they are the reward of each other. If you are a good enough man, that's the kind of woman you'll get and that's the kind of woman you deserve."[9]

Age is another friendship restriction, and generally the older people get, the fewer their friends of either sex. Booth and Hess found that the number of male friends mentioned by married women was reduced to half with advancing age, even though the overall friendship resources declined only slightly. That is, they were dependent on fewer friends. The number of females with whom a male becomes friends remains quite high as he becomes older. Because women live longer, more of them are available as potential friends to a decreasing number of older men. It was found that for women the loss of spouse is related to the limited number of opposite-sex friends reported by widows. This is because opposite-sex friends were primarily a result of marriage, and when the marriage ended, so did many of the friendships. "Thus, our prediction for unmarried persons (mostly widows) that the middle-aged would have more opposite-sex friends than the elderly is, therefore, supported in the case of females, but not for males."[10]

Another important social factor related to cross-sex friendship patterns is that of social class. In general, data from a number of countries indicate that the working classes have greater sex segregation and fewer interpersonal relationships than do the middle classes. Among the working class, the number of cross-sex friendships is even more severely restricted, because greater sex segregation and stronger "machismo" values among the men tend to devalue women and any relationships with them.

Booth and Hess found that a greater number of cross-sex friends were reported by persons in white-collar occupations and with some college education than by persons in blue-collar jobs and lacking college training. They also found status differences among women and men in their friendships. Booth and Hess further found that although men and women interacted with each other in occupational, voluntary associations and other social contexts, the interchange often had clear status differences. It was usually the male who had the superordinate position and the woman the subordinate. They found that even when the formal structure does not include status differences, the informal system tends to reinforce dominant-subordinate roles.[11] This is reflected in the fact that in many groups the men, even when there are fewer of them, emerge in positions of leadership. Generally, the men expected it and the women accepted it.

Also related to friendship across sex lines is whether or not the woman works. One study found that women in the labor force reported more opposite-sex friends than did their unemployed counterparts. Employed women often have jobs where their co-workers are males, but this varies greatly in different occupations. "The employed female's opportunities to form cross-sex friendships is still further enhanced by her membership in coordinate professional and trade associations."[12] Often the work situation for many women is so sex-segregated that there are few chances to meet men as potential friends. For example, elementary schools, clerical occupations, and nursing are overwhelmingly female worlds. A 30-year-old elementary schoolteacher said:

> My school is a disaster area when it comes to men. It's no place for meeting men to date and it's not much better for making friendships. There are four men in the whole school and one is the principle—two are middle-aged and married—and the fourth is a reject, probably even from the gay world.

Other barriers to cross-sex friendships are based on the extent to which social taboos have become internalized. If one believes it is wrong, shameful, or threatening to become friends with the opposite sex, then the chances of doing so become seriously restricted. It is not just dangers about sexual entanglements but also the belief that a relationship with the opposite sex is socially and personally demeaning, inappropriate, or wrong that stops many possible cross-sex friendships. This is more common among men than women because of traditional male beliefs about female inferiority. For some men, friendship with women is not simply something that does not occur, the opportunity should not be allowed emerge.

Women and men take different perspectives into their relationships which influence their cross-sex friendships. For example, when compared to women, men more often focus on sexuality. And men more often isolate sex from other aspects of a heterosexual relationship. They see a particular woman, or even a given time with a woman, as having only sexual significance—they show little or no interest in interpersonal involvement. Many men's idea of masculinity does not allow them to accept the notion of a long-term friendship with a woman, and as a result the only relationships they can have are short-term sexual or romantic ones. A 39-year-old salesman said:

> I think all this talk about men and women being friends is so much crap. I'm not interested in friendships with women, I get that from my buddies. Life really is very simple: men are for friendships and women are for fucking.

In general, women have been relatively more interested in and appreciative of other-sex friendships than have men. But women have also tended to be ambivalent about or dissatisfied with friendships devoid of underlying or potential love and/or sexual elements. Often, then, men and women come from different directions in what they want from cross-sex friendships, and the potential for conflict is great.

To some degree, men have always been more desirable as friends for women than have women been as friends for men. Men were the ones with the greatest power in making marriage choices. Historically, women have had few role options during their adult years other than marriage. Many women see friendship with men as a prelude to a future love relationship and the potential for marriage. Because women have traditionally been treated as inferior, they sometimes enjoy friendships with men because that represents some acceptance by men as to their being equal and worthwhile partners and companions.

The power and pervasiveness of the sexual dimension in cross-sex relationships is the result of social conditioning from an early age. Usually when a woman and man meet, their socialization leads them to respond to each other in terms of sexual attractiveness based on the many cues they have learned over the years. "Because this evaluation process takes place almost automatically, the potential is there whether or not it is consciously recognized or acted upon."[13] And because it is there it can sometimes come forth and threaten a friendship.

Many of the values about cross-sex friendships are influenced by the sexual dimension. The belief in potential sexual involvement between an unmarried woman and man probably has been the greatest deterrent to the development of cross-sex friendships. Certainly there are women and men with close friendships linked to their sexual involvement. However, it may be argued that this is difficult in many societies, including our own. The social pressures are such that if the two people like each other as friends and are also sexually involved, they generally feel compelled to move into a romantic relationship. When this happens they have a love relationship based on sexual attraction and interpersonal exchange which is socially defined as significantly different from friendship. The implication is typically that if they are not married, they should become married. If one or both are married to someone else, then the marriage(s) may be threatened by their friendship.

It is commonly assumed that a woman and man may develop a sexual relationship without any degree of friendship. However, the likelihood of friendship without sexual involvement is debatable. When it is the will of friends, the content or conduct of their relationship may be between themselves and not involve others—it is generated and stays within the exclusive bonds of the friendship. But a friendship that includes sexual involvement is difficult because of social pressures against such behavior. Privacy and exclusiveness are seen by many as important qualities of a love (or sexual) relationship between a woman and man and therefore such a relationship is often assumed to exist in almost all situations involving adults of the opposite sex. Frequently, a sexual relationship is assumed to exist between friends who keep their friendship private, whether or not it is actually the case.

Many people in interviews reported feeling the pressure of sexual involvements in friendships. Some of the women I interviewed felt that inevitably sex would interfere and threaten cross-sex friendships. A 26-year-old law student said:

> Some of my male friendships have had to end because of attempts to move it into the bedroom. I have never had one male friend who accepted the friendship without wanting to move into sexual involvement.

Another woman, a 32-year-old photographer, observed:

> I often feel like the poor little rich girl who never knows whether she is loved for her money or for herself. You meet a man and you usually assume he's after your body and not your mind. And a part of the modern male line is to applaud your intellect with lust in mind. I like sex but that's not who I am. It really makes me mad when some bastard treats me like all I am is what can be seen.

Sometimes in a friendship in which sex is involved the ending of the sexual relationship ends the friendship. But we have found a number of friendships that continued after the sexual relationship ended. One writer suggests there are special circumstances under which friendships can survive after the sexual relationship has ended. Some men and women find it easier to become good friends after they had stopped being lovers or spouses. This was often the case when sexual tension had been the cause of problems—without it, the friendship was closer.[14]

However, a number of women I interviewed told of positive values and experiences with sexuality and friendship. Four of every ten women in my study said they had wanted a sexual dimension in at least some of their male friendships and when it occurred, the experience in many cases had been good. A 25-year-old graduate student said:

> My best male friend I lived with for a year. We were lucky in that we could end the living together and sexual thing without either of us being threatened. Now we do lots of things together and are supportive of one another in our opposite sex relations.

Another study found differences between the reactions of women and men when a sexual or love relationship ended. It was found that where a rejected woman might be able to redefine her relationship with her former boyfriend from "love" to "friendship," a rejected man found it much more difficult to accomplish such a redefinition. "A couple were much more likely to stay friends when the man had been the one who precipitated the breakup (70 percent), or when the break was mutual, (71 percent), than when the woman precipitated it (46 percent)."[15]

Some persons fear that sexual involvement will threaten the friendship, and they abstain because of the threat. This appears to be a more common fear among women than men. In my study, 31 percent of the women saw sexual involvement in a male friendship as posing a real threat to that relationship. Less than 20 percent of the men had the same fear. In part, this difference is a reflection of men's greater tendency to define a sexual relationship as no longer a friendship. And sometimes men are quite willing to redefine a friendship as an affair once the sexual dimension enters.

A 37-year-old social worker said:

> To have a sexual relationship with a male friend is threatening to what has gone before in the relationship. I have had friendships end because sex entered. This is because the sexual dimension took precedence over what we had before. What happened was that once sex entered our relationship it was not kept in the proper perspective and all sorts of emotions, jealousies and so on came forth.

Another point of view was given by a 41-year-old academic woman.

> I had a friend from another department at the university. We served togethered on committees and often had lunch together. This went on for several years before we started secretly seeing each other away from school. Because we were having an affair we stopped being together as friends around the university. We were afraid that

> people would now see we were more than friends. As a result all that was left as a part of our friendship was restricted to when we secretly met. After about six months the whole thing ended–the friendship and the affair.

What do the social pressures generally imply? It can be argued that the sexual dimension is of overriding importance. Implied is the belief that if a woman and man have some dependency on each other, which is basic to friendship, they will almost inevitably become dependent on each other in the sexual area. And this sexual involvement implies, in many cases, an emotional attachment related to love. If one or both of the individuals are married, a cross-sex friendship often implies to others that something must be missing from their respective marriages, because it is generally assumed that couples will get all they need in cross-sex friendship from their spouse. This further implies needs related to different sex relationships. By contrast, a husband would not generally feel threatened if his wife had a close woman friend but often would if she had a close man friend. Often the threat is not the friendship but rather the potential sexuality.

It is clear that in all but a few relationships the possibility of sexual involvement is seen to intrude in male-female relationships. As a result, the dimension of sexuality overrides that of friendship. There is probably in many female and male relationships at least some subtle sexual dimension. They enjoy being of the opposite sex and find this attractive in each other, but it may never be manifested in sex or romance. Even this dimension, however, often runs up against social pressures, because the common assumption is that sexual expression must occur. That is, if there is even a mild sexual feeling for one another, it must burst forth or at least create problems for them. This is a reflection of the tendency to treat sexuality often as an uncontrollable drive, which is a gross exaggeration.

A 33-year-old newspaper reporter said:

> I realize the subtlety of sexual attraction is there with some of my male friends. It is a valuable addition to friendship. It is something

> that cannot be there with any of my women friends. While it has not happened to me if a good friendship should develop into a good sexual relationship I think that would be great.

A 43-year-old business woman said:

> I rely on my male friends for my sense of sexuality because that self image is given to me by men. I would be very upset if a man did not find me attractive. He doesn't have to lust after me but I at least want him to know and react in some way to my being a woman. So my relationships with my close male friends all have some sexual dimension.

The view of cross-sex friendship and the potential for sexuality varies over the life cycle. During adolescence the distinction between same-sex and cross-sex relationships becomes clear. Friends of the opposite sex are not simply friends but are "girlfriends" or "boyfriends," sometimes defensively and implying no romantic involvement—they are "just friends." Hess suggests that in old age sexuality is thought to wane, and, as in early childhood, friendships with the opposite sex may no longer carry sexual connotations.

> However, the differential mortality of males and females sets limits to the friendship formation posed by age itself. Thus the fusion of friendship with the sex role is so nearly complete through most of the life course that "friend" in popular usage, as well as in this essay, generally refers to another of the same sex.[16]

It appears fairly common to be able to combine cross-sex friendships with sexual relationships. The *Psychology Today* survey found that 30 percent of the women and 32 percent of the men in their study reported they had sexual intercourse with a friend in the past month.[17] However, those rates seem excessively high; we have no way of knowing how serious the definition of friendship was applied in those sexual experiences.

Among the men and women I interviewed I found a high recognition of sexuality in cross-sex friendships and the belief that something good was gained from at least some of the sexual involvements. Many of the women interviewed said they felt no regrets about their sexual experiences. Furthermore, a number of the women said that after the sexual dimension ended their friendships continued. Some of the women believed that the sexual experiences with some male friends was a "natural" thing to happen. The men were less likely to say they had sexual relationships with a woman friend. As was suggested, this appeared to be largely the result of men more often making distinctions between women friends and women with whom they have sexual relationships. This may be a reflection of men having less emotional involvements with their sexual partners whatever the nature of the relationship.

Other dimensions of interpersonal relationships enter into cross-sex friendships. Many men have been socialized to believe that emotional satisfaction should be sought from women, because the male role does not equip them for meeting their own—or other men's—emotional needs. Pleck observes that throughout the twentieth century men have been taught to seek their emotional gratification from women and to devalue their emotional ties with men. But in recent years men are finding that many women are refusing to play the role on which men have come to depend so much. For those who believe relationships with women are their only acceptable outlet for emotional expression, this refusal, and the feminist movement, are beginning to create panic.[18]

It would appear that increasing numbers of men find friendships with women an important means of self-revealing and gaining a greater sense of self-worth. The present study found that over a quarter of the men said they would reveal as much or more about themselves to women friends as they would to men friends. The men who saw their female friends as just as important as their male friends valued those women because of their honesty, supportiveness, and willingness to listen. These men also typically defined their feelings toward their women friends as love, affection, and warmth. They did not usually attribute those emotional qualities to their male friends. A 35-year old assistant professor said:

> My women friends are very bright, have strong personalities, a sense of humor and are also very sensitive people. They are people I completely trust. This is not something I would say about all of my male friends. With these women I would and have revealed anything to them. Not the same things to all of them but only because it has never been relevant. If anything I probably reveal too much about myself. This is something I don't do with my male friends.

Many of the men I interviewed who had close women friends saw them as emotionally closer than their male friends. A 40-year-old psychologist said:

> I have always felt I could be much closer to a woman as a friend than to any man. It is a real gut feeling I have. I feel that in general women care more about their friends than men do.

Another man, a 37-year-old lawyer, said:

> Right now, and I am sure in the future, my female friends are far more important to me than my male friends, although that was not true in the past. I am beginning to think that "macho" threatens male friendship and that is not a threat with women friends. It gets down to the bottom line of there being trust with the woman that is often not there with the man.

In her study of Harvard University senior men, Komarovsky found that their closest female friends were their primary confidantes in all areas except money. Most of the seniors were economically dependent on their parents and so turned to them as confidentes in money matters. Those men reported that the main disadvantage of a male friend as a confidante was his threat as a competitor. "A guy means competition," one senior explained. "I have competed with guys in sports and for girls. Once you let your guard down, the guy can hurt you and take advantage of you. Your girl has your interest at heart." But even with their female friends, these men did not reveal a great deal about themselves. "The seniors admitted that their lack of self-disclosure was a grievance, occasionally voiced against them, by their closest women friends."[19] It appears that often, even with close women friends, men will hold back more often than women do with friends of either sex.

As was suggested earlier there is some evidence that young and better-educated males are turning more to females as close friends. A study at Oberlin College found that the majority of males had more male best friends than female best friends, and a large percentage of them included only one or two females among their best friends. However, they tended to place greater confidence in their best female friends than in their male best friends. The same pattern held for consultation and the amount of time spent with each friend.[20] In the Komorovsky study of male university seniors, those men experienced psychological intimacy more fully in cross-sex rather than same-sex relationships. She further found that the transfer of psychological closeness from a male to female friend occurred earlier in the life cycle of males who attend college from what she found in a study done a number of years before.[21] Lopata sees greater cross-sex friendships as due to several trends. One has been the increasing involvement of both women and men in similar school and work roles prior to marriage. The worlds they grow up in are more heterosexual than in the past. The second trend has been the development and expansion of equality, companionship, and friendship in marriage between a young man and young woman sharing similar lifestyles. Friendships may increasingly be a characteristic of this kind of marriage relationship. The third trend has resulted from the upward mobility and increased affluence of a large proportion of Americans.[22] In general, this means greater equality of women and men and therefore the greater potential for friendship.

Pleck suggests there is a new pattern: Men turn more to women for close relationships, and relationships with other men are less stressed as the only "real" friendships. Pleck observes that a large number of men now report that they never had male friends. Men in my interviews said they never had a close friend of either sex in their lives. A 46-year-old business executive said:

> When I was a boy I was always a part of a gang of boys, but none of us would be "best" friend to any other. We did things together as a group and not usually just any two of us. In college I had to work hard to earn money and get good grades so I never had time for friends. I have always been a hard worker and that's meant I have never felt I had time for frivolous things—and I would include friendship in that category. I have never thought much about my lack of friendships. I guess maybe I'm the kind of person who doesn't psychologically need them—but I don't know, because these kinds of questions are ones I have never given much thought. [He laughed and went on.] I certainly wouldn't say I had any possible needs for friendship met through marriage. You could describe my marriage in a lot of ways but one sure as hell would not be as friendly.

As I have suggested, throughout this century men have been taught to attain emotional gratification from women and to devalue most close emotional ties with other men. Suddenly, many men are finding that women are beginning to refuse to play the nurturant role on which they have come to depend. As suggested in earlier chapters, women are less inclined to play this role with men because of their greater involvement and satisfaction with other women as friends. So there is a kind of irony in the male turning to the female for friendship: As men turn to women, the women may be turning away because they have established the kinds of friendships they need and want with other women. The male may be saying, "I am ready for your friendship" and the woman may be saying "I no longer have the time or the need for it." Sometimes in the past female friendships were available but men didn't want them. Today, men often want them but the women are not always available.

NOTES

1. DuBois, Cora, "The Gratuitous Act," in *The Compact,* E. Leyton, ed. (Canada: University of Newfoundland Press, 1974), pp. 29-30.

2. Smith-Rosenberg, Carroll, "The Female World of Love and Ritual: Relations Between Women in Nineteenth-Century America," *Signs,* Autumn 1975, p. 5.

3. Brain, Robert, *Friends and Lovers* (New York: Basic Books, 1976), p. 51.

4. Booth, Alan and Elaine Hess, "Cross-Sex Friendship," *Journal of Marriage and the Family,* February 1974, p. 44.

5. Ibid., p. 42.

6. Parlee, Mary Brown, "The Friendship Bond," *Psychology Today,* October 1979, p. 53.

7. Bell, Robert R., "Significant Roles Among a Sample of Australian Women," *Australian and New Zealand Journal of Sociology,* February 1975, p. 10.

8. Maslow, Abraham, *The Farther Reaches of Human Nature* (Harmondsworth, England: Penguin, 1971), p. 378.

9. Ibid., p. 94.

10. Booth and Hess, "Cross-Sex Friendship," p. 42.

11. Ibid., p. 39.

12. Ibid., p. 43.

13. Safilios-Rothschild, Constantina, *Love, Sex and Sex Roles* (Englewood Cliffs, NJ: Prentice-Hall, 1977), p. 81.

14. Ibid., p. 98.

15. Hill, Charles T., Zick Rubin, and Letitia Anne Peplau, "Breakups Before Marriage: The End of 103 Affairs," in *Divorce and Separation,* G. Levinger and O. C. Moles, eds. (New York: Basic Books, 1979), pp. 77-78.

16. Hess, Beth, "Friendship," in *Aging and Society, Vol. 3: A Society of Age Stratification,* M. W. Riley, M. Johnson, and A. Foner, eds. (New York: Russell Sage Foundation, 1972), p. 364.

17. Parlee, "The Friendship Bond," p. 43.

18. Pleck, Joseph H., "Man to Man: Is Brotherhood Possible?" in *Old Family/ New Family,* N. Glazer-Malbin, ed. (New York: D. Van Nostrand Co., 1975), p. 237.

19. Komarovsky, Mirra. "Patterns of Self-Disclosure of Male Undergraduates," *Journal of Marriage and the Family,* November 1974, p. 685.

20. Olstad, Keith, "Brave New Men: A Basis for Discussion," in *Sex: Male/ Gender: Masculine,* J. W. Petras, ed. (New York: Alfred, 1975), p. 86.

21. Komarovsky, Mirra, "Cultural Contradictions and Sex Roles: The Masculine Case," in Petras, *Sex: Male/Gender: Masculine,* p. 94.

22. Lopata, Helena Znaniecki, "Couple-Companionate Relationships in Marriage and Widowhood, in Glazer-Malbin, *Old Family/New Family,* p. 129.

6

COURTSHIP, MARRIAGE, AND FRIENDSHIP

This chapter will look at friendship for young single adults and friendship between wife and husband. For the young adult who is not married friendship may serve in some ways as an alternative to marriage—in meeting both individual and social needs. After marriage, friendship can, under some circumstances, take on threatening characteristics. These are general points to be examined in this chapter.

THE SINGLE AND FRIENDSHIP

First, I will look briefly at friendship for the single who, by definition, is out of the kinship system that comes about through marriage. Stein, in his study of single adults, has written that the greatest need single people feel when they leave the traditional family structure is for substitute networks of human relationships that will provide them with basic satisfactions of intimacy, sharing, and continuity. He found that that theme emerged in all of his interviews through the emphasis respondents placed on their friendships and interpersonal (bonding) activities. "The feeling of support from like-minded people appears to be an essential psychological condition for the choice of singlehood."[1]

Of course, being single is not always a matter of choice. Some persons choose not to marry, and others are not chosen for marriage. In general, the social pressures have long been to marry; however, this has been changing: Singlehood is becoming a more positive option to marriage, and more people are choosing it. This is reflected in the decreasing marriage rate, as well as in the fact that couples are marrying later in life. It is also clear that friends are a major resource that allow people to choose singlehood over marriage.

The single person often finds situations in which he or she relies on the family for aid or support. However, as many get older turning to the family becomes less appealing. Friends may be more important to the unmarried because they appear more appropriate. This is often true for the single in times of trouble. Edwards and Hoover write that for many single people, living completely alone may occasionally be hazardous, but often the knowledge that there is no one available motivates them to take better care of themselves. They suggest that self-reliance is one of the most important attributes for a successful life as a single person.[2] A 32-year-old woman bartender said:

> I highly value at this time of my life living alone. Living alone for me is a very positive time because I don't have to be responsible for another. I have only myself and no one else. I am sure the time will come when I will want to live with someone, but not for a while yet. I enjoy my friends—but for the most part away from the privacy of my apartment.

Certainly people who are unmarried and who live alone see fewer people than do those who are married and living with others. It is a common belief that people who live alone must be lonely. Yet, research shows that a large number of the single are not as forlorn as the myth makes them out to be. In fact, they may be less lonely than unhappily married people whose sense of isolation and loneliness can be accentuated by living with an unloved and unwanted companion.[3] Sometimes the presence of a spouse is based on a sense of duty and responsibility rather than on any positive feelings toward the relationship.

I found in my interviews that the most common description of feeling extremely lonely has come from a relationship that is in the process of ending or one which has ended. Sometimes a person continues to live with a spouse or a friend when the positive, shared experience has ended. A 29-year-old divorced woman student said:

> I really experienced loneliness with my ex-husband when we were in the process of splitting up. This lasted about six months before he moved out. He changed completely and what we once had was gone. All the ties with our shared past were broken. We would go days at a time without saying a word to each other. He would stay away more and more and when he would come home I would feel almost sick to the stomach. It was horrible.

Single people, when asked what aspect of their friendship they valued the highest, commonly reply "companionship." They describe companionship as allowing them to be themselves and do so with someone they care about and who cares about them. "Friends keep our minds alive and help us to expand our ideas. Good friends help us to define ourselves and ultimately accept ourselves."[4] A 29-year-old single man suggests that friends don't overload you with advice.

> In many ways my friends are like family, but there are important differences. They don't constantly give advice like a parent does. You can turn to them to have your needs met where with a wife or parents they give you all kinds of opinions—most of which you don't want. Basically it's that among friends you try to influence each other much less. It's not because you care less but because you all come from families and, being single, want to hear limited advice, and so when you're called on for an opinion you're careful. You know how little to give because you're often on the other side.

Edwards and Hoover point out that singles are able to rely more on their personal judgment, desires, and initiative in making friends than are married people. Furthermore, they suggest, singles are more likely to work harder at friendships, and their friends are more likely to reflect their own values and choices, since they do not have to compromise with someone else in those decisions. The friend does not have to meet the demands of two people. "Friends are the single's family–a new kind of family, one that is not built around kinship or marriage relationships but around real preference, shared interests and genuine affection."[5]

An interesting question about cross-sex friendships among single people concerns the differences between those they choose as friends and the kinds of people they marry or want to marry. One study found there to be no systematic pattern either of complementariness or homogamy of personality needs as related to selection of either courtship partners or same-sex friends.

> However, the *specific needs* and *need combinations* significantly related to selection of courtship partners or same-sex friends are considerably different. Also, the specific needs operating in male-female friendship selections are quite distinct from those of female-female relationships.[6]

The notion of love as related to friends and a spouse are described by a 36-year-old broker:

> When I think back to how I felt about my wife before we were married married and other friends, I think it was what loving each one meant. With my friends, both men and women, I cared. But there were limits on how much time I wanted to spend with them. I would want to leave them after a few hours and return to my privacy. But with my wife I realized I really loved her when I found I didn't want to leave her. I wanted to roll over and go to sleep and know she would be there the next morning, and the following morning and for all the mornings in the future.

In earlier chapters I have referred to studies of unmarried college students and their friendship needs. There is evidence that many single college men believe it is important to find a friend who is female. Hettlinger found that the most essential characteristic of a good date is her ability to make conversation, and the primary dating activity is sitting in a room talking. Out of these dating experiences emerged friendship and on other occasions increased romantic involvement. He suggests that possibly the men dated some women for sex and other women for companionship. It seems that both sex and companionship are part of the function of dating.[7] But those relationships that become friendships minimize the sex and maximize the companionship.

Booth and Hess found that unmarried persons of both sexes confided in opposite-sex friends more than in those of the same sex. However, marriage for both men and women reduces confiding behavior in all of their friendship relations. For both married males and females, confiding is characteristic of same-sex friendships more than opposite-sex friendships.[8] This is a reflection of the strong taboos against opposite-sex friendship after marriage.

Another study found that engaged males like the same type of women both as a friend and fiancee, but there was little similarity between the male friend and the fiance of engaged females. The males, in selecting women as friends, picked those who were like themselves in autonomy, deference, and heterosecuality. But the female fiancee was similar to her male friend only in the need for autonomy.

> This suggests that roles fulfilled in an engagement and a friendship by members of the opposite sex, are more differentiated for females than for males. In choosing same-sex friends women pick other females whose needs are very like their own, males select same-sex friends who are significantly like themselves only on succorance and abasement.[9]

This is further evidence of the greater importance of friendships for women than for men, and that men, more often than women, will turn to the opposite sex for the meeting of interactional needs.

Friendship as social interaction can and often does overlap with love relationships. Love may be a basis for friendship, and people may have a love relationship without real friendship. That is, people may feel a strong romantic attachment to each other but have few of the characteristics of friendship. For example, they may have few common interests and little companionship. Their focus is almost entirely in the romantic and the sexual.

There may be some reservations about speaking of friendship as a form of love because love is seen as too significant for mere friendship. Sometimes writers make a distinction between liking and loving. According to this distinction, it is normal to like our friends—in fact, that is a part of the definition of friendship. But liking is seen as less profound than loving, and loving is believed to occupy higher plateau. Of course, some people really do love their friends. Love is completely individual—it is used by different people in different ways to define their feelings toward others.

A basic characteristic of courtship choice as well as friendship choice is that we choose persons who are very much like ourselves. Like attracts like. But we also usually want something from the other that will satisfy our ego needs. In general, we are most attracted to a person who will meet our important needs. It has been argued that one of the most important is self-esteem. When these needs are reciprocally satisfied, love is typically the emotion that develops. Often the love of romance is not very different from the love frequently found in friendship. Romantic love is usually more intense, long-lasting, and sexual. The difference is less in substance and more in degree and intensity.

The personal relationships we develop are usually determined by what each individual is willing to put into it. For example, both friends and lovers typically want to conduct the interaction within the privacy of the relationship that generated it. A close relationship, by definition, is one with a high level of privacy. In the common love model in the United States, there is a call for not only sexual and affective exclusivity but also exclusive companionship. Many love relationships leave little room for any others to be close, intimate friends.[10] In general, the more intense the relationship, the greater the exclusion of all others.

The relationships between love and friendship can become confused when they are with same-sex friends. Love suggests some sexual dimension to the relationship. A 29-year-old dancer said:

> I have two very close women friends that I love very much. I have tried to discuss what I mean by this love with my husband but he doesn't understand. I think he, like many men, believe that if you talk about love between two unrelated adults it must have a sexual overtone and that bothers him. Certainly with my two women friends I feel some physical attraction but I have no desire to make it sexual in any way. By comparison when I say I love my husband I am both physically and sexually attracted to him. It is the overt sexual dimension that separates love of a woman friend from that toward a man. But I certainly feel that my emotional commitments and feelings for my friends are just as strong as for my husband. He also finds that difficult to accept because he seems to think my giving love to others somehow takes something away from him.

The idea of marriage immediately connotes commitment to another person. To become committed is to become involved and to invest oneself in that person. The ideal image of marriage commitment involves reciprocal trust and responsibility. These are also qualities common to good friendship. While the notion of love may enter friendship in marriage, it is seen as a special kind of love involving romantic and sexual components. Heterosexual love is a strong emotional attachment between those of the opposite sex with at least the components of sexual desire and tenderness. In our society to have this kind of love is to seek out marriage. When love is defined in the above terms, marriage is the next logical step. But the love of friendship recognizes friendship as completely adequate for meeting its needs.

There are similarities between friends and lovers. For example, both admire the other and do things for him or her. For both there is often a development of privacy, personal words, gestures, experiences, and so on. But, as was suggested, there are also differences. Lovers need not share many ideas or even care about the same things. Often, their love is the dominant and overwhelming force in their lives. By contrast, friendship is at its best when both partners share ideas and interests. For friends, the emotion of love may provide the meaning of many things they do and share together, but the love is usually not enough in itself.

Many years ago sociologist Georg Simmel wrote about friendship and love. He suggested that to the extent that the ideal of friendship came from the past and was developed within a romantic spirit, it aimed at total psychological intimacy. "This entering of the whole undivided ego into the relationship may be more plausible in friendship than in love for the reason that friendship lacks the specific concentration upon one element which love derives from its sensuousness."[11] The love of friendship is more diffuse than the love of romance. He wrote that friendship lacks the vehemence of love as well as the unevenness and frequent abandon. Therefore, friendship may be more likely than love to connect the whole person with another total person. But Simmel believed that this kind of intimacy was becoming more and more difficult. Modern man had too much to hide to sustain friendship as it existed in the ancient sense.

Today we hide more because there is seen to be a greater threat in revealing. In addition, modern personalities may be more uniquely individualized, and this prevents full reciprocity of understanding and receptivity, "which always after all, requires much creative imagination and much divination which is oriented only toward the other. It would seem that, for all these reasons, the modern way of feeling tends more heavily toward differentiated friendships, which cover only one side of the personality, without playing other aspects of it."[12] The love of romance is often more encompassing than the love found in the more differentiated relationships among friends.

Many people show nervousness and even strong resistance to entering a love relationship. There is often the fear of rejection, hurt, unsettling surprise, and so on. Love may not be for the security-seeking individual. "Love exposes you to unpredictability, uncertainty, and to the risk of loss,"[13] which is especially traumatic for one whose relationship ended badly or abruptly. A 32-year-old newspaperman said:

> I was living with a woman for several years and all of a sudden it fell apart. I was in a real state of shock for quite awhile. When I started to see other women I found myself offering as little commitment as possible. What I was after was to get the woman to commit herself to a greater extent than I did. What I was trying to do was set it up so that if an end occurred the hurt would be less for me than for her. I came to realize this was pretty stupid but it was for me clearly a protective device.

There are some individuals who will not risk the dangers of love in a friendship or in a romantic one. For example, there is sometimes the fear that one may project oneself as a friend and be rejected or snubbed. This sometimes happens when the individual's sense of self-worth is not high. This person is insecure about others wanting to be his or her friend. Rejection is so feared that he or she holds love back. Friendships are limited for many because they can never make the first commitment to another–there is too much risk.

One view of love is that the person has only so much to give, and that should be given in marriage. Slater suggests that the greater the love involvement, the greater the withdrawal of the individuals from society. "This accords well with the popular concept of the obvious lovers, who are 'all rapt up in each other,' and somewhat careless of their social obligations. All of the great lovers of history and literature were guilty of striking disloyalties of one kind or another.[14] It may be that persons deeply in love have a finite quantity of love that allows them to see only each other. These lovers have created their own universe, one that excludes the rest of the world.

A problem in any close relationship is the extent and acceptance of total closeness. Certainly no one can expect another to completely understand them. Each of us will always keep a part of ourselves totally private. No matter how close two people are, there is much that can never be shared. Each is so complex that he or she is not always consciously aware of this, nor can he or she find the means or have the desire to reveal everything to the other.

FRIENDSHIP BETWEEN WIFE AND HUSBAND

The high level of emotional and intellectual sharing found in many marriages is due to the fact that people can develop in those areas if they choose to and are capable of doing so. In the past in most societies, where there was less free choice in marriage the intimacy was restricted and often seen as irrelevant and even destructive to the marriage. It also had to be fairly impersonal because there was not much emotion to start with, and the relationship did not provide an opportunity for its development. Slater suggests this is why most of the great love affairs of history and fiction were extramarital. "Dyadic intimacy has often been restricted to the more voluntary extramarital relationship."[15] Great love affairs had emotional openness not found in marriages of the time.

In my research on friendship between husband and wife, only about one-half of the women named their husbands as a very close friend. About 60 percent of the married men named their wives as a very close friend. Greeley argues that marriage is a friendship, and if it is not a friendship it is not a satisfactory human relationship.[16] If he is right, we would estimate that at least one-half of all persons who are married have unsatisfactory relationships.

However, people want certain things from marriage and are willing to put up with situations they are not happy with to gain them. For example, the freedom from loneliness that is often derived from marriage may more than compensate for stress. Glenn writes that

> if men, on the average, experience less stress from marriage than women, it seems likely, in view of the happiness data, that they also derive less pronounced positive effect, so that the balance of positive and negative psychological consequences is similar for males and females. In other words, it is likely that women, as a whole, exceed men in both the stress and the satisfactions derived from marriage.[17]

This would suggest that women are more likely to experience friendship in marriage or strong hostility than are men.

Marriage provides many needs of friendship between spouses as well as outside the marriage. In general, same-sex friendship outside the marriage are not encouraged. This is because in modern marriage they are often seen as threatening to the marriage by competing for time, attention, and fulfillment of needs. "However, sex-segregated worlds in marriage still exist as ideals among some ethnic groups and among the less educated, particularly in cultures emphasizing 'machismo' maleness which would be corrupted by too close contact with women."[18] In those settings the main friendships with other men are seen as totally separate from marriage and, in some societies, as far more important.

As was discussed, some persons view their spouses as best friends, while others do not. And this is probably more common for men than women, because men have fewer friends outside marriage. A 36-year-old academic man said:

> I think I am very lucky. I consider my wife to be my very closest friend. We enjoy doing many of the same things. But what is most important is we like to talk to one another. It's like when you are out in a good restaurant and you look around at the couples. You can tell those who are married because they have little to say from those who are not married, at least to each other, because they have lots to say. Even though we have been married for 12 years we like to think that our level of talk is such that when we leave people will say there go a couple who are not married to each other.

A 41-year-old woman antique dealer also feels good about her husband as a friend.

> I feel my husband is definitely my best friend. I would reveal anything to him. I feel strongly that I love with my husbnad because I want to, not because I have to. If I had to I know I could handle all the practical matters of life by myself. But I sometimes wonder if I need his emotional support to survive. Because he is so important as a husband and a friend I really fear the future possibility of losing him.

However, there are a number of women and men who express different views about spouses being friends. A 36-year-old insurance saleswoman said:

> It's hard for my husband and I to be friends because we are so different. For example, I can be at a whole table of people and still be miles away. I'll pick up portions of the talk but still be off in my own little world. I feel very comfortable with this desire to draw within myself. But my husband is the opposite and he needs people all the time. So I often feel like I am letting him down when I withdraw. I realize there is a level of selfishness in this. But if I can't be good for myself I can't be good for anyone else. I try to work out my needs to be alone when my husband is away or doing something.

> But most of the time when he is around and has nothing else to do he wants the friendship of marriage. We are both trying to compromise our different needs—but I don't predict success.

A 44-year-old businessman said:

> I don't think that friendship has anything to do with marriage. I wouldn't want my wife to be my best friend. I think as a wife she should respect me and treat me the way a good wife should. For my friends I want other men who can share activities with me and opinions that a woman can't. I believe that a woman's world is different from mine and that's as it should be whether she is my wife or any other woman.

An important part of the American values that center on romantically based love in marriage has stressed the belief in the wife and husband being friends. As Lopata points out, wives and husbands in America are supposed to be best friends and no other adult relationships should interfere with the fullness and complexity of the ideal modern marriage.[19] This often implies that all interpersonal needs met through friendship can be better met through marriage. It would seem that this view places an extra burden on marriage. I found in my interviews that it is not common for women to be friends with their husbands to the exclusion of all other friendships. This appears to be more common among the husbands, but most of them also have friends outside marriage. Wives and husbands typically see their spouse as a friend but each also sees others as friends. In general, the friendships outside marriage are presented as having little to do with friendship with a spouse.

There is often a strong pressure in marriage, often during the first years, to end friendships outside marriage and turn within for meeting those emotional needs. Frequently early in marriage the commitment and expectations for the romance are overwhelming and seem to include everything. But usually with time the expectations become more realistic and decrease, and the interpersonal dimensions expand outward from marriage. As I discussed in an earlier chapter, this is often the case where the friend is married to someone else, especially one of the opposite sex. Not just marital partners, but also relatives and acquaintances sometimes find it hard to accept the existence of such friendships. "Spouses particularly resent them because of the existing close ties and the sharing of experiences, even when they are convinced that there are not sexual or love elements." 20 The reaction of jealousy is described by a 45-year-old accountant:

> My wife used to have a friend at work and she would often have lunch with him and they would also talk together at other times. It really bugged the hell out of me. This was true even though what they shared in common was of no interest to me. But I think what really got to me was that she would tell me a lot of the things he would say and he would come across as profound or witty. He was finally transferred to another office and if she has any new male friends like him she now keeps it to herself.

Over the years it has been common for many writers to argue that in some ways the amount of time and emotional energy available to sustain close relationships must be finite. The belief is that one's ties to the family will affect, and be affected by, the existence and strength of other ties. Therefore, if one spends "all" one's time and emotion with kin, there is little left for neighbors or other friends.[21] Shulman goes on to state that the principle that close relationships must be cumulative and have finite amounts of time, needs, and emotional energy, if accepted, leads to the expectation that those with marriage partners will have fewer needs to be met and less available time for involvement with other intimates. "The greater involvement of single young adults within their networks, as compared with middle-aged, married people is supportive of this principle."[22] However, I do not find this to be true when age is held constant. In fact, the evidence suggests that the opposite may be true—that is, people who have high marriage and family involvement also have high involvement with friends.

What is particularly important about the above point is that the psychological and social nature of individuals that leads them to want to interact with people is the crucial variable. If having relationships with people, whether kin or friends, is highly important, then people will find the means to do so. One woman, a 38-year-old high school teacher said:

> I consider myself to be a very busy person. I have my job, my husband, and two teenage children. It seems to me that we do more together as a family than most others that I know. But I also have good friends and it is true that sometimes we would like to get together more. But when that's not possible we use the phone.

The evidence suggests that many friends of married persons are couples rather than individuals. These kinds of friendships will be looked at in the next chapter. A majority of the married people I interviewed said they have friends of their own not shared with their spouse. But these respondents are middle- and upper-middle-class people and would be biased in the direction of more friends outside marriage. By contrast, in a more random sample of older women, Lopata found that 92 percent of the prior-to-widowhood friends are identified by the woman as having also been the friends of the late husband.[23]

NOTES

1. Stein, Peter J., "Singlehood: An Alternative to Marriage," *The Family Coordinator,* October 1975, p. 501.
2. Edwards, Marie and Eleanor Hoover, *The Challenge of Being Single* (New York: Signet Books, 1974), p. 48.

3. Ibid., p. 47.

4. Ibid., p. 118.

5. Ibid., p. 116.

6. Hendricks, Jon, "Leisure Participation as Influenced by Urban Residence Patterns," *Sociology and Social Research,* July 1971, pp. 250-51.

7. Hettlinger, Richard F., *Human Sexuality: A Psycho-Sexual Perspective* (Belmont, CA: Wadsworth Publishing, 1974), p. 49.

8. Booth, Alan and Elaine Hess, "Cross-Sex Friendships," *Journal of Marriage and the Family,* February 1974, p. 45.

9. Banta, Thomas J. and Mavis Heatherington, "Relations Between Needs of Friends and Fiances," *Journal of Abnormal and Social Psychology,* 66: 50 (1963).

10. Safilios-Rothschild, Constantina, *Love, Sex and Sex Roles* (Englewood Cliffs, NJ: Prentice-Hall, 1977), p. 97.

11. Simmel, Georg, *The Sociology of Georg Simmel* (trans. Kurt H. Wolff) (New York: Free Press, 1950), p. 325.

12. Ibid., pp. 325-26.

13. Douvan, Elizabeth, "Interpersonal Relationships: Some Questions and Observations," in *Close Relationships,* G. Levinger and H. L. Rausch, eds. (Amherst: University of Massachusetts Press, 1977), p. 22.

14. Slater, Philip, "On Social Regression," *American Sociological Review,* June 1963, p. 349.

15. Ibid.

16. Greeley, Andrew M., *The Friendship Game* (New York: Doubleday, 1971), p. 311.

17. Glenn, Norval D., "The Contribution of Marriage to the Psychological Well-Being of Males and Females," *Journal of Marriage and the Family,* August 1975, p. 599.

18. Lopata, Helena Znaniecki, "Couple-Companionate Relationships in Marriage and Widowhood," in *Old Family/New Family,* N. Glazer-Malbin, ed. (New York: D. Van Nostrand Co., 1975), p. 127.

19. Lopata, Helena Znaniecki, *Women as Widows* (New York: Elsevier, 1979), p. 205.

20. Safilios-Rothschild, *Love, Sex and Sex Roles,* p. 97.

21. Shulman, Norman, "Life Cycle Variation in Patterns of Close Relationships," *Journal of Marriage and the Family,* November 1975, p. 813.

22. Ibid., p. 820.

23. Lopata, *Women as Widows,* p. 217.

7

MARRIED COUPLES AND THEIR FRIENDSHIPS

Marriage has come to mean that social relationships are to be shared between couples. The common pattern in the middle class has come to be that each person may have some friendships with members of the same sex, but any friendships with the opposite sex will be within the context of married couples. Married couples typically constitute the basic unit with respect to primary friendship relations in the American middle class. Babchuk found that is there a tendency not only for spouses to see themselves as a unit in the friendship network but for their friends to see them in the same way.[1]

It is probable that friendships between two married couples rarely give the exclusiveness and privacy of close friendship between two persons. The very fact of having four people involved makes it difficult. Friendships between married couples typically may be subdivided into close friendships between the two husbands and the two wives. It is not common to have the subdivision of close friendships between the two wives and the two husbands who are not married to each other. In fact, very often when two couples get together, it is in reality two sets of friends getting together—the two women and the two men. Frequently the corss-sex interactions are superficial and ritualistic.

Often the view of social interaction after marriage implies a kind of symmetry, a need for balance that is achieved through having even numbers of both sexes. A great amount of adult social life is based on pairs—the pairs of marriage or other opposite-sex combinations. The ideal balance is a woman for each man and vice versa. That balance is reflected, for example, in the seating of persons at a dinner party: The host or hostess hopes the same number of women and men will attend so they can be seated alternately. But if there is one extra woman or man the balance is thrown off.

Couple friendships are also influenced by the marital status of their friends. Babchuk and Booth found that single females had less difficulty in confiding in the husbands of close friends than did wives in confiding to single male friends.[2] This is probably a reflection of the greater restriction on married women against any type of involvement or revealing to another man regardless of his marital status. There is simply more support for the married man to confide in other women than is true for married women to confide in other men.

The kinds and intensity of relationships outside of marriage clearly have an impact on the role relationships of marriage. One study found that when husbands and wives belong to same-sex friendship groupings outside marriage, it is within that setting that much of their general values and ideas about the relationships of men and women occur. In this regard, extra-familial social relationships can strongly influence conjugal roles. But where there is an absence of extensive social relationships outside marriage, such as one-sex groups, "which can provide important social support functions, spouses will become more interdependent and consequently forced into a more joint relationship."[3] Often a fairly concentrated involvement with same-sex friends not only provides a good deal of social involvement but also reduces the defined need for some of the interpersonal demands of marriage.

As was discussed in Chapter 5, there is always the potential for sexual or romantic involvement when the opposite sexes are involved in friendships. With couple friendships, this tends to be minimized because they are doing things as couples, and usually when they are paired off it is woman to woman and man to man. But among some couples there may be some mild flirtation. This typically occurs in the open and in front of the respective spouses. If it becomes more isolated and hidden, the potential for jealousy and conflict often increases. This point is illustrated in the comments of a 52-year-old businessman:

> There are two couples my wife and I are friends with. On a weekend we all get together and go out for dinner. Or sometimes to a nightclub or stay home and play cards. We have known each other for years and there is a certain amount of sexual teasing by the men. It's nothing serious and it's all out in the open and everybody laughs. I sometimes wonder why, because we have been saying the same things for years. Generally, when all of us are talking together, it's not serious—we tease, tell jokes or make remarks about other people. Some serious discussions take place among the men and, from what my wife tells me, among the women.

He was asked if any pair, not married to each other, had ever gone away from the other four on their own. He said,

> yes, that has happened a few times over the years. Once when we were all on a weekend vacation I went for a walk with one of the other women and we were gone for several hours. When we got back the air was a bit frigid. So I would say it happens once in a while but it certainly is not encouraged.

There can often be a tugging between friendships and marriage relationships. Ideally, the friendships among married couples will enhance their respective marriage. But in some instances, the friendships and marriage may be in conflict, and one may be destructive to the other. Sometimes people try to substitute through various kinds of friendships what they feel they are lacking in marriage. This is illustrated by the married man who turns to another woman with the assertion, "My wife doesn't understand me." Often the motive is "will you provide me with what my wife won't?" Of course, this is often a tired old line of an attempted seduction.

There are different patterns for the development of couple friendships. Typically one partner brings along the other couple for his or her spouse to meet and accept as a possible friend. Babchuk found that there was consistent support for the hypothesis that the husbands initiate more mutual friendships for the couple than do wives. "Typically, husbands and wives not only agreed on who initiated the friendships listed by both but further agreed that it was the husband who was dominant."[4] Often the couple friendships come through the husband's interests, frequently through his work. This means that the two men often have the common experiences of similar occupations and often of even working together. They usually start out with much more in common than do their wives. Traditionally it has been assumed that the wives can make do in friendship development on nothing more than their common experiences as wives and mothers. Rarely would men be expected to develop a friendship around nothing more than their common experiences as husbands and fathers.

A 42-year-old woman described her experience of making couple friendships.

> When I look back, most of the couples that have been our friends were initiated by my husband. Those would usually be men he worked with. I would call and invite them over and of course the other woman and I would be strangers. It was always assumed that we would find something in common. The few times I tried to initiate new friendships with couples, but my husband was not cooperative. This was because the other man did something different in work and my husband would say they wouldn't have anything in

common. The assumption has always been the women can find something in common. But for the men there must be something already there or no friendships.

The husband is influential in couple friendship formation in other ways. Babchuk found that very close friends of the male in the period prior to marriage were more likely to become mutual friends of the couple after marriage than were very close friends of the female. "Also mutual friends developed subsequent to marriage are more likely to be introduced to the pair by the husband rather than the wife."[5] Babchuk further found that before and shortly after marriage single individuals predominate in the network of primary friends of both spouses. But after marriage as friends of the husband are likely to become friends of the wife, she orients herself away from her own primary friends during the period of engagement. "This shift takes place in the courtship period, a period in which the male more often determines the kinds of activities the couple will engage in, where the couple will go, and more importantly for the present analysis, with whom the couple will associate. Male superordination continues for as long as the couple is married but is more pronounced in the early period of the marriage."[6]

Early in marriage there may be conflict over friendships, especially among working-class women toward the friends of their husbands. Rubin, in her study of working-class families, found a major concern of the young wife was to break her husband's attachment to his high school peer group. She also found that often the husband objected to the friends his wife brought into the marriage. The husband "complains often that he does not like her high school girl friends or that their husbands aren't his 'idea of a guy I want to bother with.' "[7] This also illustrates the general point that men are less willing to expand their boundaries with regard to possible friends; they are more conservative about developing new friendships than are women.

The fact that married women have been traditionally restricted to the home has limited their opportunities for meeting a variety of persons out of which friendship might emerge. Gillespie found that women who moved to the suburbs for the first time found they were more dependent on their husbands for a variety of services previously provided by members of tight-knit networks. "The wife frequently regrets the move to the suburbs, despite more pleasant living conditions, because of its disruption of the kinship and friendship network."[8]

In part because of the greater restrictive social nature of women's lives, they generally have more friends than do men. When the woman is restricted to the home and her contacts are limited, friendship becomes of increasing importance. Because she has a more limited range of potential friends to choose from, those contacts that do exist take on greater importance. And because she is often restricted to the home and community, she needs those women who are in situations like her own. Therefore, the development of friends takes on a high priority; she attempts to develop as wide a range of friends as possible.

One study of middle-class wives in Great Britain found that the general pattern of their social life was a fair amount of entertaining and a good deal of visiting with their female friends during the day. Friendships were important and served to indicate "how middle-class wives were able to maintain a fair degree of independence, outside their roles as mothers, during the period when the children were young."[9] The nature and extent of friendship for women varies over their life cycle and also the age cycles of their children. To the extent that young children tie the mother to the home and the immediate neighborhood, her friendships tend to come from that restricted area. When the children get older and enter school, her friendship circles broaden somewhat.

Lopata found that women active in voluntary associations are likely to bring into their marriage friendship groups people they met at meetings. "Urban working women in their twenties are the most apt of all women to draw their friends from work situations. Neighbors provide friendship opportunities, particularly for couples tied down in their range of movement by small children or lack of resources."[10] But these sources of friendship represent a relatively small part of all couple friendships.

In American society, regardless of who makes the initial contact, it is usually the function of the wives to provide the continuity for socializing.

> The degree of closeness finally developed within couple-companionate friendships seems to vary considerably according to such factors as social class, which prescribes the rules of etiquette and the amount of social distance, the age of participants, competition from other social roles, and social relations, and personal characteristics and wishes.[11]

But it is generally the woman who serves as social secretary and arranges when couples will meet and where and what they will do.

Husbands and wives do not always agree on the friends they have in common or each other's individual friends. Babchuk and Bates found that 39 couples in their study 277 friendship units. Of that total, both spouses agreed on 118 friendships, but the husbands reported 87 friendships not mentioned by their wives and the wives reported 72 not mentioned by their husbands. "The striking fact was the paucity of close mutual friends shared by husbands and wives."[12] They also found that while respondents included the spouses of very close friends as members of a primary group, those spouses were not as close as the friend. Only rarely would both spouses be viewed as equally close friends by the party making the judgment. "Husbands were most likely to exchange confidences with men and wives with women, but husbands found it easier to exchange confidences with the opposite sex than did their wives."[13]

The above study would suggest that couple friendships are not balanced, that frequently two people have the friendship and the other two go along with it. Most often the friendship is between the two husbands; the friendship interests of the women are somewhat less. This seems likely because the men are more likely to be the initiators of the friendship and also because women's friendships have traditionally been defined as less important than those of men. Often in the past, not only men but also many women defined the expectations for women's friendships to be less and for that to be the way it should be.

It has been suggested that the couple friendships formed jointly by a husband and wife have less intimacy than the more exclusive close relationships of only two people. This appears logical when we keep in mind that the needs and demands of four people will be much more difficult to meet in a satisfactory way than when there are only two people involved. It may also be that couple friendships are based more on utility than on strong emotional commitment. That is, couples get together more to do things with or for each other than to meet the emotional needs of one another.

It would also appear that couple friendships change over time as individuals grow older. On the one hand there seems to be a decrease in couple friendships because there is often a declining interest in shared social activities with another couple. And with age there is often an increase in interests and activities that are more sedentary and solitary. This also implies less involvement with one's spouse over the years. On the other hand, because as couples get older they are less involved in activities with friends and with each other, their friends may come to be valued more for their helpfulness and dependability. Orthner found a tendency for roles to be increasingly divided over the years of marriage and for separate interests to develop. Thus, there is "a rather steady decline in jointly shared leisure activities over the marital career."[14] This is true for the married couple and for their relationships with other married couples.

What is often important to couple friendships is how people see themselves and their relationships to others. Babchuk found that most of the time husbands and wives saw themselves as a unit vis-à-vis other friends and believed that their friends saw them as a pair. "There were instances, however, where the husband singled out a married male as a close mutual friend and where the wife would include the same male *and* his wife on her list."[15]

A 38-year-old housewife describes her marriage as the unit of friendship.

> A great deal of our social life we do as a family. My husband, children and I go camping in the summers, take other kinds of trips, go to the movies and eat out together as a family. Our activities with our friends are always with other couples–John doesn't go out with the 'boys' and I don't go out with the 'girls.' We really are a partnership in our social activities and this is also true for our friends. We all tend to think of each other not as John and Mary but rather as the Smiths."

Friendships among middle-class couples can take place on different levels. As described by Lopata, couples may organize their friendships in various layers. She describes this as ranging from one or two couples whom they see most often and with whom they feel closest to an outer layer of the "crowd," which gets together periodically for large parties. The younger women defined the five couples they saw the most as their closest friends. But they also believed that old friends cannot be replaced. Lopata says this may be due partly "to the fact that past friendships can undergo a process of idealization or even sanctification, as in past marriages in the case of many widows, making current levels of friendship undervalued."[16]

The 38-year-old owner of a small business describes the levels of friendship on which he and his wife are involved:

> There are a group of about eight couples who make up our crowd. Lots of times, especially during the winter, we all go to the same

> parties. None of us are really close friends but there is a kind of security, a feeling of belonging, to this kind of relationship. You always have something to do on Saturday night and how everyone will behave has already been established. Those who will drink a little too much, or flirt or insist on singing are predictable. Truthfully, it often gets boring—but its the only action around.

Hess suggests there is evidence that married couples constitute the visiting units for the weekends and evenings even though that does not necessarily imply agreement of friendship choice among marriage partners.

> Thus, visiting friends may be an activity of the married pair, but an individual choice of "best friend" need not be dependent upon his spouse's choice. Rather, it seems most fruitful to view the married state as a condition under which certain other persons are available as friends; whether or not these become close friends depends upon other sets of variables, social and psychological.[17]

The weekend sets up special demands. For many Americans it is the time to do something, and in the middle class this often means with other couples. The weekend is the time for entertaining; for married couples, that usually means with other couples. Often weekend friends are people to do something with, to entertain, and by whom to be entertained. While a best friend may be a part of a couple one does something with on a weekend, it is not usually on the weekend that the closeness and intimacy of the friendship will be drawn upon. In addition, weekend couples who are friends are "specialized" friends—couples with whom to play bridge or tennis.

It is of interest that the interpersonal relationship of the couple often becomes the basis for their intercouple relationships with others. But what is seen as very basic to the interpersonal relationship—love and sexual attraction—is viewed as inappropriate, and potentially highly destructive, to interpair relationships. Therefore, when couples come together as friends, it is understood that certain things will not happen. The severity of these restrictions is much greater than between paired friendships, whether they be of the same sex or of the opposite sex. The sanctity of marriage must be preserved.

SOCIAL CLASS

As was previously suggested, friendship patterns are related to different social class levels. The evidence indicates fewer friendships of all kinds in the working class than in the middle class. Komorovsky found that joint social life with friends was not nearly as important a leisure-time pursuit among blue-collar couples as it was in higher socioeconomic classes. "This applies to exchanges of home visits as well as to joint visits to public recreation places. About one-fifth of the couples never visit with another couple apart from relatives. An additional 16 percent do so only very infrequently, a few times a year." Komorovsky goes on to observe that even those who do maintain social relations with other couples have a small circle of friends. "For one-half of them this circle consists of only one or two couples. Only 17 percent see as many as four or more different couples in the course of a year."[18]

Another study found that in both middle- and working-class marriages about 40 percent of the women said they did not spend evenings in the company of friends away from their husbands. But the middle-class women did indicate that they and their husbands had more friends as a couple than did the working-class women.[19] In a study of working-class women in Great Britain, it was found that 25 percent of the wives said that neither they nor their husbands had any friends at all. The 35 percent who reported having many friends were referring to persons they visited in the evenings, and most of them said those persons were also friends of their husbands.[20]

There are also sex differences in friendships within the lower class. One study found that in working-class marriages the wife tended to maintain close ties with relatives and old girlfriends, while the husband continued to associate mainly with his friends from before marriage. Often for the woman social and psychological support came not from her marriage partner but from her kin. The friendships of the working class women are not only more localized and circumscribed than those of the middle-class woman but also more localized than those of her male counterparts in the working class.

Working-class women compared with middle-class women are much less likely to speak of friendships. In addition, their general leisure-time activities are much more restricted. Lopata found that often the working-class woman's social interaction was restricted to her neighborhood, and that was only if the neighborhood was defined as friendly, which it often was not. Mostly those women's leisure-time socializing was limited to relatives or religious events.[21]

Lopata provides insights into why so many working-class women have so few social relationships. She points out that most urban Americans are still first-, second-, or third-generation immigrants of lower socioeconomic background. Their culture has not included intense socialization into any subculture of polite companionship. Lopata goes on to say that most working-class Americans do not engage in formal, event-focused, "friendly" interaction, such as dining by invitation at home (or in other locales), game-playing, or just conversation.[22] Rubin found in her study of the working class that generally it is the relationships with extended family—parents and siblings—that are at the heart of working-class social life. "Partly this close relationship with extended family inhibits joint friendships with outsiders since it fills both the time available and the need for social relationships."[23] But these are also the relationships that are most "natural and right" to the working class.

As I noted, working-class men probably have less involvement with both kin and friends than do working-class women. Often men establish some kinds of social relationships with other men they work with, but, unlike in the middle class, this does not usually provide a basis for bringing the friendships home. Rubin found that "sharing friends and entertaining at home still is not a commonly accepted part of working-class life."[24] This was especially true for men.

While for many working-class men there is a level of involvement with other men, it often does not imply a deep level of interpersonal commitment. Certainly it is an important part of their leisure-time involvement, and it may occupy many hours every week. But it is often not friendship in the sense of strong interpersonal relationships. This point is made by a 32-year-old semiskilled worker:

> I have lots of buddies. A buddy is a guy you can have a beer with and kibbitz around. We mostly talk about sports and cars. To answer your question, I don't think of these buddies as really close friends. I don't have any close friends and neither do most of the guys I know. I think a friend is a guy you get close to, someone you can really unload with. But that's not part of my life and I don't feel like I am missing anything. With buddies it's all out in the open and you don't owe anybody anything.

KINSHIP AND FRIENDSHIP

In this section I want to examine briefly how kinship and friendship function to meet interpersonal neds. As discussed in Chapter 1, in most societies kinship relations have met the needs of the individual, but this is often no longer the case in modern American society.

In the United States kinship has come to have a more restricted meaning. It appears that many kinship ties further removed from those of adult children and their parents lack any real feelings of closeness and identification. Adams found that the sibling contact among a majority of the young adults in his sample did not manifest the characteristics of social companionship. Rather, it consisted of home visiting, communication, and family ritual occasions. "The question 'how am I doing' can be quickly and readily answered by comparing oneself with his sibling or siblings. Such rivalry or comparison appears crucial, particularly in brother relations, even in adulthood." Adams goes on to say that when one looks toward cousins and other secondary relatives, one is hard-pressed to find any great significance in those relationships. He did find a tendency to add as intimates other kin as substitutes for a missing relationship. "If an adult has no children, he is close to his nephews and nieces; if he has no siblings, he may be close to his cousins."[25]

It has long been recognized that women have more involvement with kin than do men. The maintenance of kinship ties and the arrangements for their continuation are generally thought to be the special province of women. For example, Adams asked his respondents, "How important are kin in your total scheme of things?" The majority of his female respondents felt that "kin were among the 'most important' aspects of their lives (58 percent), while the largest proportion of males (49 percent) saw kin as 'somewhat important,' but not as of 'central importance' to them."[26]

Typically in the working class the couple relationships are with the wife's family. A 37-year-old assembly-line worker said:

> I like to stop and have a couple of beers with my friends. That's usually Friday and it's payday. Once a week I go bowling. My wife doesn't have any friends other than her mother and two sisters. Usually on Sunday we go to her folks' for dinner. Her old man and me sit and watch whatever games on TV—we sit and have a few beers. He's always talking, saying things like "did you see that?" or explaining what's going on. I sometimes wonder if he thinks I'm fucking blind or something. But he's not such a bad ol' fart and he really has had to work his butt off his whole life. My mother-in-law keeps my wife off my back because she listens to her complaining and bitching about the kids. And that saves me from listening.

Komarovsky, in her study of blue-collar marriages, also found greater kin contact for women. "Only 43 percent of the husbands, but 62 percent of the wives, enjoy 'close' relations with their mothers. The proportion of 'close' relations with the father is 34 percent of the wives, and only 27 percent of the husbands."[27] Another study found that women reported more close kin than men. "Women maintain intimacy with parents and siblings as well as their family of procreation; men tend to restrict primary kinship relations to their family of procreation."[28]

The women Komarovsky studied reported two reasons why they and their husbands had more association with their parents: The women had the greater attachment to their parents, and they were in the dominant role of planning social activities. But this caused no problems, and the men accepted the women's decisions as proper for kinship interaction.[29] Another writer suggests that a reason for the greater closeness to female relatives can probably be explained by the fact that women tend to act as the representative of the nuclear family in fulfilling obligations. "The central role of the woman in performing duties imposed by kinship apparently also provides opportunities for her to show preferences for the maternal side of the family despite the normative pattern of treating maternal and paternal relatives equally."[30]

There are some differences in the emotional ties of kinship and friendship. The friend may be epitomized as the social companion, while the kinsman is the object of continuing interest. Adams found that, generally, interaction is likely to be desired with friends rather than with kin, due to the consensual component of friendship and the absence of strong obligatory feelings toward friends. So consensus and affection may be the essence of close friendship and affectional or positive concern the dominant characteristic of intimate kinship.

> In order to account for kin bonds we therefore postulate a form of interpersonal attraction based upon positive concern, or the interest

> of one individual in the well-being and activities of another. This attractional factor, we repeat, explains much affection and contact in the social network, particularly with kin, apart from either consensus or sheer necessity.[31]

The research on kinship, friendship, and social class indicates that the lower classes have less contact with friends and possibly even less with kin. There is also evidence that members of the middle class are more likely to keep their kinship and friendship networks separate. Bott found that among middle-class persons many of their friends did not know each other, and it was unusual for friends to know relatives. In that group ties were maintained with only a few relatives, and the husband and wife had little contact with neighbors.[32] Babchuk found that frequent association with relatives did not predict what the pattern of visiting with friends would be.[33]

Some couples may feel a strong desire to keep their family separate from their friends. This appears to be fairly common when the couple has moved up the social scale. They may take on a new lifestyle very different from how they were reared and are embarrassed by the old values. This feeling is described by a 39-year-old psychologist:

> I have always made an effort to be sure that my friends never met my parents. I feel guilty as hell about that but I sure can't deny it. It's not too difficult because my parents live 800 miles away. But once on a Saturday night we were having dinner at our house with two couples who were good friends and my parents unexpectedly appeared. I was really uptight because I was afraid their manners would be sloppy, their grammar bad and their Midwestern values as right wing as ever. And sure enough they lived up to my worse fears.

In turning to kin and friends there are various psychological factors involved. Certainly, many people confronted with a choice will openly choose friends over kin. Adams, in his study of young adults, found that 43 percent said they favored contact with friends, 27 percent favored kin, and 30 percent would like to equalize time spent with the two groups.[34] Another study found that friends and neighbors were three times more likely to be nominated as sources of emotional support than parents. "Further data . . . showed that religious ministers, priests, doctors were a more important source of emotional support than siblings to parents."[35] Many who have been well socialized to the role of the family meeting all interpersonal needs may feel guilt in turning to others.

Given the voluntary nature of friendship, there are important differences for maintaining relationships with kin and friends. Most of the respondents in Shulman's study said they maintained their relationship because it was enjoyable. A significant number also said that obligation and need were important reasons for maintaining contact. But obligation and need were more frequently applied to kin relationships than to friends.[36] In general, friendship is not an obligatory relationship.

Clearly, in many areas of life friends are seen as more understanding and supportive than kin, probably because of shared experiences in which family members cannot take part. A 33-year-old nurse said:

> There are many things my women friends can give me that my family can't. We have experienced many of the same problems and can be comforting to each other. We have all had problems in marriage and with rearing children. But we have also lived through a period of many changes in the roles of women that can best be understood by our own age peers.

It therefore seems reasonable to assume that many persons will turn to friends to discuss things they choose not to discuss with kin. Often the choice of a friend is based on similarity of interest. There are sometimes problems that should be withheld from the family. For example, a person will choose to talk to a friend about sexual matters because he or she believes such a subject is not appropriate to discuss with kin. This point is illustrated by the remarks of a 28-year-old woman:

> There are so many things I would not discuss with my mother. I will ask her advice on the kids or on running the house. But when it comes down to my personal life, no. I would be embarrassed to do so. So I have a friend I can talk to about my husband and sometimes about sexual things. My friend and I are at the same stage of life so we can relate to each other. But my mother is my mother and all that implies. And she is also of another generation.

NOTES

1. Babchuk, Nicholas, "Primary Friends and Kin: A Study of the Associations of Middle Class Couples," *Social Forces,* May 1965, p. 491.
2. Babchuk, Nicholas and Alan Booth, "Voluntary Association Membership: A Longitudinal Analysis," *American Sociological Review,* February 1969, p. 40.
3. Wimberley, Howard, "Conjugal-Role Organization and Social Networks in Japan and England," *Journal of Marriage and the Family,* February 1973, p. 128.
4. Babchuk, "Primary Friends and Kin," p. 492.
5. Ibid., p. 484.
6. Ibid., p. 486.
7. Rubin, Lillian Breslow, *Worlds of Pain* (New York: Basic Books, 1976), p. 198.
8. Gillespie, Dair, "Who Has the Power? The Marital Struggle," *Journal of Marriage and the Family,* August 1971, p. 88.
9. Gavron, Hannah, *The Captive Wife* (Harmondsworth, England: Penguin, 1968), pp. 103-4.
10. Lopata, Helena Znaniecki, "Couple-Comanionate Relationships in Marriage and Widowhood," in *Old Family/New Family,* N. Glazer-Malbin, ed. (New York: D. Van Nostrand Co., 1975), p. 137.
11. Ibid., p. 128.
12. Babchuk, Nicholas and Alan P. Bates, "The Primary Relations of Middle-Class Couples: A Study in Male Dominance," *American Sociological Review,* April 1963, p. 277.
13. Ibid., p. 278.
14. Orthner, Dennis K., "Familia Ludeno: Reinforcing the Leisure Component in Family Life," *The Family Coordinator,* April 1975, p. 179.
15. Babchuk, p. 487.

16. Lopata, "Couple-Companionate Relationships," pp. 128-29.

17. Hess, Beth, "Friendship," in *Aging and Society,* M. W. Riley, M. Johnson, and A. Foner, eds. (New York: Russell Sage, 1972), p. 363.

18. Komarovsky, Mirra, *Blue Collar Marriage* (New York: Vintage Books, 1967), pp. 311-12.

19. Simon, Rita James, Gail Crotts, and Linda Mahon, "An Empirical Note About Married Women and Their Friends," *Social Forces,* June 1970, p. 523.

20. Gavron, *The Captive Wife,* p. 98.

21. Lopata, Helena Znaniecki, *Women as Widows* (New York: Elsevier, 1979), p. 208.

22. Ibid.

23. Rubin, *Worlds of Pain,* p. 197.

24. Ibid., p. 198.

25. Adams, Bert N., "Occupational Position, Mobility and the Kin of Orientation," *American Sociological Review,* June 1967, p. 377.

26. Adams, Bert N., "Isolation, Function and Beyond: American Kinship in the 1960's," *Journal of Marriage and the Family,* November 1970, p. 579.

27. Komarovsky, *Blue Collar Marriage,* p. 312.

28. Booth, Alan, "Sex and Social Participation," *American Sociological Review,* April 1972, pp. 189-90.

29. Komarovsky, p. 245.

30. Robins, Lee N. and Miroda Tomanes, "Closeness to Blood Relatives Outside the Immediate Family," *Marriage and Family Living,* November 1962, p. 345.

31. Adams, Bert N., *Kinship in an Urban Setting* (Chicago: Markham, 1968), p. 68.

32. Bott, Elizabeth, "Urban Families, Conjugal Roles and Social Networks," *Human Relations,* 8: 363 (1955).

33. Babchuk, p. 488.

34. Gibson, Geoffrey, "Kin Family Network: Overheralded Structure in Past Conceptualizations of Family Functioning," *Journal of Marriage and the Family,* February 1972, p. 22.

35. Shulman, Norman, "Life-Cycle Variation in Patterns of Close Relationships," *Journal of Marriage and the Family,* November 1975, p. 817.

36. Ibid., p. 818.

8

DIVORCE AND FRIENDSHIP

In most instances separation and divorce are not sudden breaks, but rather steps in a process. All of the actions and reactions between the two people takes place over time. With time comes the realization that the marriage is going to end. In varying degrees, at different times for different individuals, other persons play a part in the divorce process–children, family, and friends. But often for the person entering separation and divorce there is a strong sense of failure and loss. One consequences of this is that, regardless of even close kinship ties and warm friendships, the person will often feel isolated, because the divorce causes either or both partner to look within him/herself to deal with the failure of a relationship that was initially entered with the assumption of success.

Often the most shocking aspect of ending a marriage is the initial separation. This involves moving away from not only what has been the physical setting of one's life for some time but also an interpersonal setting that for at least a while was emotionally satisfying. Fear appears to be a natural reaction for persons facing or experiencing separation, fear about what is left behind the prospect of starting all over again. Divorce deprives a spouse, for varying periods, of the partner on whom he or she relied. For those who have been married for some time, the separation can be especially frightening. Most frightening is the unknown, not knowing what to expect. One recently divorced 36-year-old woman said:

> For a long time my marriage was terrible. I wanted out of it so much but I was so frightened. I had so many fears of what it would be like with my three children "out there." Many of my fears were not even rational. But when I finally did move out I found that most of my fears were not real and I really regretted waiting so long."

As a marriage undergoes the changes that move it into separation, each partner is constructing his or her own reality of the marriage. Initially the need may be to construct an account in order to explain the breakup to oneself, but very soon it is also needed to explain what has happened to one's family and friends. This is a major part of the social process of presenting to the world a marriage that is ending. And because the reality of the divorce is usually different for the two people, their accounts of what led to the divorce are different.

One often hears about vindictive and nasty separations and divorces where the two people attack one another. Weiss found that more often the pattern is a kind of unspoken agreement about what will be said and not said about the partner. This usually includes the assumption that one partner will not broadcast embarrassing information about the other or demean him or her in front of others. But Weiss found that in the failing marriage the expectation of the partner being trustworthy was sometimes broken in both small and large respects. For example, sometimes the husband or wife would tell friends damaging stories "in confidence" and the friend would pass it on.[1]

Epstein points out that there is both a community and a psychic divorce being carried out at the same time—that is, what is happening in the community view of the divorce and what is happening in the psyches of the divorcing couple. At the same time they are trying to establish new autonomy in the community, they are often trying to cope with their new single status. "Having to take on both these problems at once—that of reestablishing one's social life while coming to terms with oneself emotionally—is often what makes the early months, and sometimes even years, after divorce in many ways so grueling."[2]

In general, divorce involves more problems for the woman than for the man. Traditionally the woman has had fewer options to marriage and therefore its loss is often more threatening. Albrecht found that divorce was perceived as more traumatic by women than by men. The most common factor that made the divorce traumatic and stressful was a feeling of personal failure. But for a majority, once the decision was made to go ahead with the divorce, things got better.[3]

However, men appear to undergo the greatest initial shock with separation because they are usually the ones who leave the familiar surroundings of home. As a result of the move, men often feel a lack of identity, a sense of rootlessness, and they complain that there is a lack of structure in their lives. Epstein found that feelings of loneliness and being lost are common among divorced men. The most common of all their thoughts and fantasies was a return to the marriage, "of picking up the pieces and putting everyone's life back together again."[4] A 35-year-old male lawyer said:

> For the first six months after I moved out I used to spend many hours in my apartment daydreaming about moving back home. I found I was so used to having my wife around that I even missed her irritating me and making me angry. It was the silence of my apartment that got to me. I wasn't really lonely but I wanted the routine of my life to return—even though it had often been miserable.

Part of the pattern of adult life is for the man to have less family involvement than does his wife. Therefore, when he gets a divorce, he has fewer established kinship ties on which to rely.

And the male, more than the female, will feel it inappropriate to turn to his kin for emotional support. As a result, he is more likely to turn to his friends for support. But given the fact that men generally have fewer friends than do women, they, much more than women, have to go it alone after separation.

Studies show that after separation how the individuals are able to adapt is significant for what they can do in their lives. Spanier and Casto found that persons who had difficulties adjusting to a new style of living without the spouse reported "depression, loneliness, frustration, low self-esteem and self confidence, as well as heightened negative feelings toward and regrets about their (former) spouse, marriage and separation."[5]

Sometimes couples separate, announce to their families and friends that a divorce is to take place, and then go back together. But although they have reconciled, their friends and relatives may see them in a somewhat different light because the troubled marriage has been brought out into the open. And many such reconciled couples separate again; however, kin and friends may not show great concern this time, assuming the couple will once again reconcile.

It is common in a failing marriage for one of the partners to try a variety of strategies to reinforce it. Sometimes even hostility is used in interpersonal relationships as a last-ditch effort to salvage the relationship. People who are deeply committed may feel that any intimacy is better than none and recognize intuitively that when all else fails attack is likely to bring forth a deeply personal reaction.[6] Hostility at least represents an emotional response as compared to the indifference that indicates rejection.

Recent years have seen the occurrence of the "friendly divorce." Weiss points out that this kind of divorce has its poignancies and may ask of the couple generosity they may not have shown in their marriage. But it can provide them with the belief that their years together were not wasted. Implied is that even though they are separating, they can, within limits, still count on one another. "Unfortunately, more separations seem to be at the other extreme, with one spouse or both acting as the other's enemy and persecutor."[7] For a divorce to be friendly, generally it must not be perceived as threatening to either partner, that neither feels rejected and both look forward to what lies ahead. When that happens the divorce can be seen as a neutral, if not a positive, experience.

It is likely that most couples are too angry and upset after their marriage ends to be even polite and civil to one another. For them the notion of a friendly divorce is impossible; based on their negative experience, they find the prospect of seeing each other, let alone remaining friends, distasteful and even unnatural.

Weiss found a few couples that remained friends after their separation. Those couples would talk to each other often and spend time together, especially with their children. There were other couples who felt an increase in friendliness with their spouse after separation, but they often had mixed feelings about it. The new friendliness was often bittersweet—painful as well as sometimes rewarding. "It carries unhappy memories and is itself a remainder that things might have been different and better, if only the couple had been able to be friendly earlier."[8] But maintaining a close relationship after divorce is the exception to the rule. Albrecht found that once the divorce was obtained, neither males nor females reported much continued contact with the former spouse. "More than 7 out of 10 of the respondents reported that they had little or no contact with the former spouse."[9]

As was suggested, when separation and divorce occur, the person turns to kin and friends as resources. Traditionally, although kin provide help in most situations, divorce is not one of them. Kinship systems have always highly valued the sanctity of marriage, and divorce is a relatively recent phenomenon. As a result, when people turn to kin at the time of separation, the family, upholding traditional values, attempts to persuade the couple against the divorce.

Not only do family members tend to take a more restrictive view about marriage than do friends but they also believe it is their right, not friends', to make judgments and to try to influence behavior. "Parents, especially, assume the right to comment on the separation, to criticize it, to disapprove or approve it, perhaps going on until the separated individual is driven to exasperation."[10] A 35-year-old accountant said:

> My family's reaction to my news that my wife and I were getting a divorce was to say in effect "go back and try harder." When I tried to explain that we had been "trying harder" for a couple of years their reaction was to go back and *really* try hard this time. I left their house really pissed off because I knew I wasn't going to get any support from them–and I didn't.

By contrast, one of the important qualities of a good friend is that he or she is nonjudgmental and tries not to impose his or her own values. This is in part why people getting a divorce will more often turn to friends than to kin for psychological support.

It has also been found that families and friends of separated couples react differently to their new lifestyles. Friends usually accept whatever postmarital relationships individuals establish, while the family often holds them to what it believes to be proper, irrespective of the wishes of the separating persons. This appears to be especially true for the woman–her family, more so than the man's, insists on defining the propriety and appropriateness of whatever pattern of life she chooses. Although she is an adult, her family will often assume it should oversee her morality once she no longer has a husband to do so.

Once separation and divorce occur, women more often receive assistance from their families. This is because their resources are fewer than the man's and they have a greater need for day-to-day help. It appears that women who are best able to cope with their families and the help they receive have a network of friends on which to draw. The friends not only provide social supports but also give the woman a sense that what she is doing is alright. With her friends she can usually be her new self in her new role, while her family often expects her to be as she was—what she no longer is or can be.

Many women who become separated and divorced are caught in a very difficult position. For many of them, marriage continues to be seen as the major, if not the only, role a woman should play in her adult years. When she no longer plays this major role friends can become especially important: they constitute a group of significant others who support her in her new role.

The usual first reaction of friends to the news that a person is ending his or her marriage is to show solicitude, regret, and a desire to be helpful. But as time goes by, while some of the friends remain loyal, others withdraw. In part this is because some friends from the person's married years cannot adjust to his or her separation or divorce. The friendship often assumes marriage, so without marriage the friendship loses its reason for being.

The reactions of friends to the news of divorce can vary greatly. Friends who are not very close are likely to be the most surprised by the news that a couple has separated. Sometimes even the most intimate friends are not told until the separation is very near. "Tact and good form, and a natural desire to avoid embarrassment should the separation not occur, require that couples keep their troubles to themselves."[11]

Sometimes the outward form of a marriage is retained because of the fear of the divorce's effect on friendships. If a person fears that friends will not be able to handle the divorce, he or she may withhold the news as long as possible. There is also the possibility that because a marriage fails, the couple may think they are incapable of making or keeping friends. A 33-year-old divorced woman commented:

> We really didn't develop any close friends in the three years of our marriage. I think that is something that happens in bad relationships. You don't want others to see how things are for you. It's hard to get together for fun when you don't feel anything good toward the person you are married to.

There is some evidence that among women in the lower socioeconomic classes the impact of divorce is even greater on their relationships than in the middle class. One study of low-income mothers found that their relationships with friends outside the family suffered following divorce.

> One-fifth of that sample seemed to have no outside friends at all. In part this may be a reflection of stronger conservative values against divorce in the working class. These women may be in a double bind with regard to friends after divorce when compared with middle class women. They have fewer friends to start with and lose more of those they have because of value differences about divorce.[12]

As the separation takes place and friends learn about it and have the chance to respond, the divorced person often develops a process of selecting relationships. The divorced woman comes to lose contact with those who do not sympathize with her troubles or who do not give her the warmth and friendship of old ties. "By the time the divorce has occurred, her circle has become a sympathetic set of friends and relatives for the most part, having gradually lost those who expressed antagonism toward the breakup."[13]

Often divorce means the reduction of some contacts with kin and friends. Albrecht found that the most common pattern was not one of withstanding and imposing isolation on the self after divorce. Rather, the most common response was to report a decline in participation during the first year followed "by no appreciable long term change in level of social participation as a consequence of the divorce action."[14] The decline in participation is often due to the new role demands of being divorced. But once the person becomes more at ease with the new role, new relationships can and do occur.

As suggested, often after separation friendships drift apart. Spanier and Casto found that for the most part when friends grow apart after separation, the person who was separated was just as responsible–perhaps even more so–for the split as are the friends. The separated person may no longer feel part of the group. "Occasionally they also reported feeling that they were a threat to married couples, either because they represented the possibility of marital failure or, more directly, because they might be considered a sexual threat."[15] This same study also reported that the growing away from friends after separation was especially true if the friends had been shared with their spouses and particularly if the friends were also couples. It is no longer a couple to couple friendship but rather an individual to couple relationship, which is often difficult to maintain.

Contact with divorcees, as was suggested, may stir up personal conflicts in the friends about their own marriages. They may withdraw friendship from the divorced person because of guilty satisfaction from knowing their own marriage is secure. Miller observes that a friend's response to a divorce has to be seen in terms of whether or not the idea of divorce, the reasons for it, the way it is carried out, and the emotional results threaten the friend's psychological defenses against anxiety. How the person reacts in the face of the divorce can be seen as responses to the threat.[16]

There is often an element of intrigue to divorce for friends. While some may see the divorce as a threat to their own marriages, others will experience guilt or even vicarious shame. Still others may find in the divorce the fulfillment of their own secret wishes. "The 'plot' of a divorce–who was the initiator, who opposed it, the presence of a third party–is also important to the attitudes friends take."[17] Often the picture of the divorced person's life has little to do with reality. A 32-year-old business executive said:

> After I had been separated for a couple of months I found some of my male friends really had a wild image of what my life was like as a new bachelor. They would keep telling me how I was making out and how every weekend I must be taking a different woman home. When I insisted that I wasn't they thought I was putting them on. Believe me, I wasn't kidding. I wished I was, but I sure wasn't.

It has also been found that in some groups of friends divorce can become contagious. Once one in the circle of friends gets a divorce, the new is no longer new and any feeling of shame has been greatly reduced.

> The standard of behavior might, in fact, swing in the opposite direction, where divorcing takes on a positive significance. When the standards are ambiguous, the divorced couple might be viewed in a critical light, and become the scapegoats for the friends' struggles with their own internal ideals and acceptable forms of coping with conflict.[18]

With separation and divorce the person takes on new social roles. Often the implications of this change are mysterious: some become fantasy-laden and can become a target for a friend's projections and identifications. "Friends may imagine that the separated person is having a marvelous time or a terrible time, on the basis of their fantasies of what their life would be like if they were single again."[19] It is often easy to shift from fantasizing about what the separation is like for the friend to what it might be like for oneself. The effect of this may be that a divorced person's friend who is contemplating separation considers it more seriously.

Rather soon after separation, married friends begin to see the separated person moving into a new way of life. How they respond will be in terms of how they relate the separation to their own marriages. Often the behavior of friends to the divorce situation is determined mainly by their emotional reactions. Sometimes they may encourage the divorce quite openly and in other instances the encouragement may be more subtle. Miller observes from his study of people who have been divorced that their friends may show any of the following: (1) anxiety, (2) shame, (3) inordinate preoccupation with divorce, (4) desire about the divorcee's suffering, (6) feelings of superiority, (7) surprise and incredulity, (8) emotional loss and grief, (9) conflict over allegiances, (10) disillusionment about friendship, (11) crisis about personal identity, (12) preoccupation and curiosity about the settlement.[20]

Hunt, in his study of the formerly married, found that at the time of separation and for a while thereafter most married friends were sympathetic and tolerant as well as supportive and helpful. But this often changed with time, and it was painful for the divorced to find that even their oldest and dearest friends lost their sympathy and tolerance and became cooler as the divorced person became more adept at living and enjoying his or her new life. "The same couple who applauded his dating and early involvements slowly changed over the years; the smile becomes chilly, the enthusiasm turns to condescension."[21]

Friendship may end when there is recognition that the separated person's life is now different and that the friendship is less rewarding than it once was. The friendship may not end abruptly, but fade away. Sometimes the separated blame their married friends because they imagine themselves to have been rejected unfairly by those friends. The importance of the support of friends is reflected in the research finding that nonsupportive friends make adjustment—particularly emotional adjustment—to separation more difficult.[22]

Sometimes the reactions of friends can seem to the separated person as aggressively nurturant. "They hover about, as though the separated person had become critically ill and they were the only medical personnel in miles."[23] A 34-year-old divorced college student said:

> I think everyone else knew before I did my husband was running around. Everyone knew, but I didn't. Everyone went through the shock before I did. So for them when the divorce came it was expected. Sympathy, always sympathy. I started to resent it. I thought everyone was pitying me. It was sort of their looking at me like this horrible thing had happened and I had nowhere to go and my life was ruined. I resented this and when I started to work I dropped those friends.

In general, the greater the feeling of unhappiness about the separation, the greater the need for friends. Friends who can tolerate the person's unhappiness can sometimes be of real help. Their home can be a haven. But friends who are married can also increase the feelings of loneliness by intensifying the divorced person's feeling of being marginal. The most difficult time for the separated person may be at the end of the evening when they must go home alone.

One study found that divorced women living in the more affluent suburbs complained of loneliness and isolation but did not feel that their neighbors criticized them or made moral judgments about them. "Most people who act cool to you do it out of a sense of not knowing what to say, not knowing what to do, or out of a fear of talking with you because they see in their own marriages some of the things that were in your marriage, which are probably in every marriage."[24] Another part of the problem is that there is no clear social reaction for responding to the news of a divorce. If a person you haven't seen in some time tells you he or she is now divorced, how do you react? Do you offer congratulations or condolences?

While support from family and friendship is basic to divorce adjustment, also of importance are the person's inner resources—the extent to which they can turn within themselves. For many, this can help to make the aloneness of divorce a positive experience. One woman, a 29-year-old nurse, said:

> Since I have been divorced I really value my time alone. Sometimes I turn down dates and going out just so I can stay home to read or listen to music and draw. I find it hard to convince my friends that I really want to stay home alone.

Others may isolate themselves after divorce because they do not want to be around others. Spanier and Casto found that some respondents who isolated themselves said they did so because they did not feel like being social. One said, "those that are happy, I don't want to go near. They make me feel terrible." Others said they felt like a "third wheel" or that their couple friends might consider them a "threat" now that they were single. "Whatever the reason for isolation from friends or family, we found that those persons who did not make friends had a very difficult time adjusting."[25]

Weiss found that sometimes social isolation could give rise to a form of loneliness that was almost as painful as the loneliness of emotional isolation. "The symptoms include feelings of exclusion, of marginality produced by rejection because there is no one to share one's concerns. Daily tasks may lose their meaning."[26] A 31-year-old woman said:

> After a marriage of nine years I found that our mutual friends seemed to treat me differently because I was a single woman and was not related to as a part of a couple. I felt alienated somehow and then very disappointed and all the time lonely in that I no longer seemed to have any friends. But this did turn out to be a major turning point in my life because I got over my fear of meeting people and found new friends on my terms.

There is some evidence that loneliness after divorce may be more common to men. In most instances the man moves from home and for at least some time lives alone. By contrast, while women often feel isolated within their communities, the degree to which they feel that isolation seems to depend on a variety of factors. Older age, lower incomes, and fewer friendships appear to be related to divorced women's feelings of isolation.[27]

As discussed in an earlier chapter, most friendships of married couples are with other couples. Divorce ends the couple to couple, friendship, although an individual can remain a couple's friend. A couple seriously considering separation and divorce may avoid social interaction with other couples. Their conflict may be such that they dislike planning things together so they stop asking their friends to their home. And friends who are aware of the conflict may also hesitate to socialize with the troubled couple.

The separated couple may discover that some friendships depended on their marital status. Separated persons may discover that they have been a member of a social network that was limited to other married couples. Often separation destroys their social life. It may be the network of married friends, more than specific friendships, which are the casualty of divorce. Over time there may be continued friendship with one or two married couples but a loss of access to the network of married friends. With the loss of the network may come the loss of a sense of membership in a community of friends, and with this can come the discomforts of social isolation.[28]

Some friendships in marriage exist through the spouse. For example, after divorce, the husband may lose touch with the couples he met through his wife's work contacts or other activities. The wife will lose contact with her husband's co-workers and their spouses. Probably the loss of any friends, regardless of how initiated, hurts to some extent. This is true even when the friends were primarily the spouse's friends. And when the friend makes a choice for the ex-spouse, this can be very upsetting. A 35-year-old man said:

> There was a couple that I thought were equal friends with my ex-wife and myself. When my wife and I separated I knew that these friends were going to be caught in the middle so I didn't see them for awhile. I was later stunned to hear through a mutual friend that they said I was a real bastard and the cause of the breakup. I finally called and got the woman on the phone. She quickly told me she didn't want to talk to me because of how rotten I had been to my wife. She hung up on me. They never wanted to hear my side. Maybe it's easier for people not to hear two sides–then you don't get caught in the middle.

Because most couple friendships are initiated by one or the other of the partners at the start, it often makes a difference in which one will remain friends after a divorce. And any individual friendships that are formed by the person in marriage usually remain theirs after the divorce. Weiss found that work relationships and friendships based not on the person's life situation but rather on his or her personal interests or qualities (for example, bridge) would remain relatively undisturbed by separation. The woman could also expect to retain their neighborhood friendships made among the community of women left behind when their husbands went off to work. "That their particular husbands will no longer return in the evening will not especially effect these friendships, unless it becomes suspected that their new availability is a threat to neighborhood marriages."[29]

Often after separation and divorce there appears to be little reason to retain friendships with some married couples. This may be because the common bonds of interest, often based on two married couples, no longer exist and there may not be enough left to make friendship worthwhile. Or it may be that after divorce an evening spent with married friends may force the separated individual to recognize how much his or her life has changed. Albrecht found that the divorced discovered that most of the social activities of friends were couple-oriented and that they had become an extra person–which was often uncomfortable and embarrassing.[30]

Sometimes for divorced women new problems emerge with old male friends. The woman finds herself receiving romantic and sexual advances from a man who never acted that way before. For many men her divorced status makes her more sexually desirable and available. The divorced woman can find the sexual advances of a long-time friend upsetting. A 38-year-old divorcee said:

> One man, a friend of my ex-husband's and mine, called me after the divorce. I was startled to have him come on in a way totally different from before. He was trying to hustle me at a time I still thought of him and his wife as both being good friends. He came on with inviting me away for a weekend. I felt some hurt but mostly angry. I had heard that men did this after a woman was divorced but I didn't think it would happen to me with any of my male friends. I was so furious I told him to fuck off. That not only ended the relationship with him but also with his wife.

After separation and divorce as one leaves behind some friends it becomes increasingly important to develop new friendships. In general, the more interaction the separated person can have with friends, both old and new, the fewer adjustment problems they will have. Often the person seeks out new friends to meet new needs. They may be concerned with their new status, and friends can help them learn their new roles and new lifestyles.

Sometimes the person will have developed new friends before the separation takes place. Spanier and Casto found that a number of separated persons had already developed their own circle of friends before the separation. But whatever the situation, those who did have an intact network of friends found their adjustment much easier; those who were losing old friends but were unable to make new ones found the process of adjusting to separation much more difficult.[31]

As I have suggested in earlier chapters, the young adult appears to have more skills in developing new friendships than do older people. Regardless of marital status, it was found that the younger women were more skillful in developing friends and using community resources than were older widows. "The friendships of the younger women were shaped by their desires to make their own decisions about their own lives and then to make them work."[32] Evidence shows that the higher the education of the woman, the more likely she is to have a circle of friends after divorce.

To some extent, divorce takes the person outside the family system. Even the woman who keeps her children and has contact with her family is still outside the family to the extent that she no longer has a husband. This means than fewer family contacts of any type, and the divorced person therefore looks elsewhere for supportive relationships—to friends. It may also be that the person is rejected from at least some family contacts because he or she is divorced. One divorced woman, a 29-year-old student, said:

> I developed new friends with other divorced women. No one in my family had ever been divorced. Those new friends made it sort of acceptable. But I still felt kind of guilty because I was the first to divorce in my family. They also had children and I saw how they handled them as divorced mothers and that helped me.

While the new friendships after divorce are of great importance, they do not alleviate all feelings of distress over the end of the marriage. And while new friendships can help ease many strains, they cannot resolve the disruptions that often occur with kin, children, and even old friends. It may also be that sometimes new friends are made with haste because of the desire to fill gaps from the past. Like marriage on the rebound, there can also be friendship on the rebound. Such friendships may not last, or, while they last, may not prove to be rewarding. As a result, some divorced persons have to deal with a second set of failures in some friendships. Successive failures can threaten the self-confidence of a person who already has some doubts about him or herself and interpersonal abilities.

The development of new contacts and possibly new friendships can be important to the divorced woman with children. The new relationships not only provide some emotional support but also set up an exchange of goods, services, and advice. Often the new friends make an important contribution to the day-to-day living of the divorced mother. They can share child care and the transportation of children. At this stage there may be practical considerations on choosing a new intimate friend. It may be another woman who is in the same situation or an acquaintance who some time before had separated and divorced. Often it is the common bond of the separation experience that brings women together as friends. "There may be recognition that the friendship, though important, is a product of shared extremity, like the relationship of combat buddies."[33]

While turning to other separated and divorced persons may be to receive help, there are also other reasons. Divorced women and men find that developing friendships with other divorced people often provides a sense of membership in a community—a community of divorced people. It can be helpful to the individual entering that community for the first time to find how many others there are like him or herself. A 38-year-old professor describes part of his world of divorce.

> I have been separated and divorced now for three years. When I think about my friends I realize that most of them are new since I got divorced. Also in most situations the women I have dated and had any involvement with have also been divorced. I have found that the common experience of divorce is a positive bond. I was at a dinner party not long ago and there were six of us. We discovered that all of us were divorced and as soon as that was recognized you could feel a really positive feeling around the dinner table. I have

> also found that often divorce transcends sex status. What I mean is this. If you get a group of divorced men together or a group of divorced women each group will tend to cut up their ex-spouses as a group of men or a group of women. But when you have a mixed group of divorced persons the sex difference with regard to the spouse doesn't usually matter. I can bitch about my ex-wife and get sympathy from the divorced women and they can tell me what bastards their ex-husbands were and get agreement and sympathy from me.

I have found some divorced people who say they have always made a deliberate attempt not to develop new friendships with other divorced people. A 28-year-old secretary said:

> I am not, and never have been, into developing relationships with other women who have also been divorced. My two best friends are married and have very good marriages. I have never tried to build friendships on the basis that another woman was divorced, too. In fact, I have felt negative about that. It may be that my values are not really with divorce but rather with marriage although I didn't have a good one.

After divorce a special friendship may develop—a confidante relationship. A confidante is one who is brought much more into the personal problems than is often the case in friendship. Divorce can be a time when the person needs a confidante relationship to satisfy the need to turn to someone trustworthy and caring.

Frequently the demands of being divorced leave little time for developing a new social life. The newly divorced woman has the responsibilities of raising children and taking on new jobs. Or she may not want to develop new friendships. Bequaert suggests that women may not feel like engaging in a social life, but may seek necessities or even substitutes for that which sustained them in their marriage.[34] A 31-year-old divorced woman said:

> After my divorce I was left with two small children and a new full-time job. I found that my new life was so busy that I had very

> little time to myself and practically no time for friendships, old or new.

Longfellow found that "the single mother is solely responsible for all the tasks and family maintenance [and this] may mean that she simply does not have time to be in contact with other supportive adults."[35]

Divorce may lead to changed concepts of friendships in other ways. While married, one usually had some friends of one's own and friends one shared with one's spouse. After divorce, one can select friends without consideration of anyone else. Kohen, Brown, and Feldberg point out that once she is no longer "half a couple," the divorced woman can make her own decisions about the friendships she wants or needs. When the women in that study were asked if they lost any friends because of divorce, several answered as did the following woman. "Lose friends? No, because they weren't my friends, they were his. Now my friends are different–more intelligent, active people who do things."[36]

After divorce there are various resources to which people can turn for interpersonal associations besides family and friends. For example, there are a variety of formal organizations in the community. Albrecht found that males were more likely than females to report that their participation in clubs and organizations was unchanged or higher compared to when they had been married. While the women reported a lower degree of participation in organizations, they also reported significantly more contact with relatives than was true before the divorce. "For females, then, the change was more likely to be family-related while for the males it was extra-family related."[37]

Organized attempts have been made to help persons deal with divorce through semiformal organizations. The best known of these is Parents Without Partners (PWP). One study suggests that women but not men found this group valuable because it provided them with the opportunity to form same-sex friendships with those in similar positions. Many of the women had given up friendships they had made during their marriage because of differences in schedules and interests. "The new friendships that developed were most likely to be established by women of similar age and socioeconomic status who lived near enough to one another to be able to visit occasionally and exchange such favors as babysitting."[38]

Weiss found that PWP is easy for new members to enter. Many of those in the friendship networks were themselves in a new member's situation or recently had been. Within the larger organization there was also likely to be an ideology of friendship toward newcomers. Often the organization functioned as a refuge from daily frustrations. Services were offered that were designed for the potential members' needs. For example, children's activities were scheduled for Sunday afternoon so that men who had their children had somewhere to take them. However, some members expressed defensiveness in belonging to PWP—they may have seen their reliance on the organization as a reflection of their own lack of resources.[39]

Once a person is divorced, he or she moves into new relationships with the opposite sex. There is now the opportunity for cross-sex friendships with and without romantic dimensions. Because of negative experienes with a spouse, there may be a strong desire to not get romantically involved, and therefore the person seeks the opposite sex for "just friends" relationships. But dating becomes significant, and making a date may be reassurance that one can be successful with the opposite sex. A 45-year-old man said:

> After you spend years in a marriage being put down as not worthwhile and as not being a very attractive human being your self-image is damn low. It was really a great surprise to find that some women didn't see me that way. I was really surprised to find how easy it was to make dates and have a good time. I at first thought this can't really be me—I must be dreaming.

While it may not be intended, sometimes a friendship that develops after divorce may be only temporary, lasting only until a romantic relationship comes along. Weiss found that when the new romantic relationship developed, often the new intimate friendships were permitted to fade away. The new friend felt grief and resentment at being dropped.[40]

Ultimately most divorced people remarry—about four out of five do so. The chances are greater for men—about five-sixths—than for women—about three-fourths. Half of all remarriages occur within three years of divorce. Persons who divorce and remarry are about as satisfied with their second marriage as are persons with their first marriage.

Remarriage can often have implications for the ex-spouse. It tends to decrease any friendly feeling and involvement with the ex-spouse. As Epstein points out, it is not that most divorced people wish ill of their remarrying ex-spouses, but they don't like the idea of that the other may find greater happiness than they themselves have. Furthermore, when an ex-husband or ex-wife does find happiness after divorce, this implies a criticism of the former spouse.[41] But whether a person remarries or remains divorced, it is doubtful that many couples remain friends after their divorce.

NOTES

1. Weiss, Robert S., *Marital Separation* (New York: Basic Books, 1975), p. 30.
2. Epstein, Joseph, *Divorced in America* (New York: Penguin Books, 1974), pp. 234-35.
3. Albrecht, Stan L., "Reactions and Adjustments to Divorce: Differences in the Experiences of Males and Females," *Family Relations,* January 1980, p. 62.
4. Epstein, *Divorced in America,* p. 232.
5. Spanier, Graham B. and Robert F. Casto, "Adjustment to Separation and Divorce: A Qualitative Analysis," in *Close Relationships,* G. Levinger and H. L. Rausch, eds. (Amherst: University of Massachusetts Press, 1977), p. 226.
6. Douvan, Elizabeth, "Interpersonal Relationships: Some Questions and Observations," in Levinger and Raush, *Close Relationships,* p. 27.
7. Weiss, *Marital Separation,* p. 67.
8. Ibid., p. 91.

9. Albrecht, "Reactions and Adjustments to Divorce," p. 65.

10. Weiss, p. 132.

11. Ibid., p. 150.

12. Longfellow, Cynthia, "Divorce in Context: Its Impact on Children," in Levinger and Rausch, *Close Relationships*, p. 296.

13. Goode, William J., *After Divorce,* (New York: Free Press, 1956), p. 166.

14. Albrecht, p. 64.

15. Spanier and Casto, "Adjustment to Separation and Divorce," p. 224.

16. Miller, Arthur A., "Reactions of Friends to Divorce," in *Divorce and After,* P. Bohannon, ed. (New York: Doubleday, 1970).

17. Bequaert, Lucia H., *Single Women Alone and Together* (Boston: Beacon Press, 1978), p. 84.

18. Miller, "Reactions of Friends to Divorce," pp. 66-67.

19. Weiss, pp. 158-59.

20. Miller, p. 71.

21. Hunt, Morton M., *The World of the Formerly Married* (New York: McGraw-Hill, 1966), p. 249.

22. Spanier and Casto, p. 217.

23. Weiss, p. 159.

24. Bequaert, *Single Women Alone and Together,* p. 82.

25. Spanier and Casto, p. 218.

26. Weiss, p. 163.

27. Bequaert, p. 85.

28. Weiss, p. 162.

29. Ibid., p. 153.

30. Albrecht, p. 64.

31. Spanier and Casto, p. 224.

32. Bequaert, p. 85.

33. Weiss, p. 242.

34. Bequaert, p. 94.

35. Longfellow, p. 297.

36. Kohen, Janet A., Carol A. Brown, and Roslyn Feldberg, "Divorced Mothers: The Costs and Benefits of Female Family Control," in *Divorce and Separation,* G. Levinger and O. C. Moles, eds. (New York: Basic Books, 1979), p. 241.

37. Albrecht, p. 67.

38. Weiss, Robert S., *Loneliness* (Cambridge: MIT Press, 1973), p. 215.

39. Weiss, *Marital Separation,* p. 245.

40. Ibid., p. 242.

41. Epstein, p. 224.

9

THE ELDERY AND FRIENDSHIP

Traditionally, the family has been the setting for meeting the physical, social, and psychological needs of the elderly. But with industrialization, the care of the elderly was taken over by other institutions. The emergence of Medicare, social security, and housing developments for the elderly have helped place the older person outside the care of the extended family. All of these changes imply a reduction in the interpersonal relationships that have been common to the extended kin system. How the interpersonal relationships for the elderly have been greatly changed and how their needs are now being met are the main interests of this chapter.

For Americans over the age of 65, about two out of three men are married and living with their wives. But only one out of three older women are married and living with her husband. About two-thirds of all older people who are unmarried live alone. Those who live alone include one of seven older men and one of three older women. And for most of those elderly, living alone is a recent experience, brought about by the death of a spouse of many years.

There are strong advantages for those older persons whose marriage remains intact. Marital satisfaction is positively related to higher morale for older people. This relationship also appears to be even stronger for women than for men. Furthermore, better health is correlated with high morale, and both are correlated with marriage.

Marriage appears to play a more central role in the older woman's social life as well as her overall assessment of her situation in life than it does for the man. The loss of a spouse through death has a greater negative impact on the psychological well-being of men than women. It is harder for men to deal with life after the loss of their spouse. "It seems to be the case that, in terms of morale and related variables, men are more responsive to the simple presence of a spouse, while women are more sensitive to variations in the quality of the marital relationship."[1]

In many respects, remaining married into old age has definite gains. For the married there is the positive effect of psychological well-being among the elderly, especially when compared with the divorced and widowed. There is also reason to suspect that overall levels of marital satisfaction and adjustment may be higher for the elderly than the married people in the intermediate stages of the family life cycle. This may be due partly to fewer options for close relationships. Children are grown up and gone, the man is often retired, and both spouses may be more physically restricted. As a result, the marriage takes on greater importance. Of course, this can also place a heavy strain on the marriage.

In the past, heavy reliance was placed on adult children in caring for aging parents. But this is much less true today. Turning to one's children is not an option for all of the elderly. For example, eight percent of all persons over age 65 have never been married. Furthermore, married persons who had children, may have outlived their children. Of the total noninstitutionalized population over 65, about 25 percent have no children. While some of these persons may have siblings to whom to turn, many older people in effect have no kinship structure in their lives. Certainly, as the extended family of cousins, aunts, and uncles continues to shrink, it means fewer kinship relationships available to persons at all ages.

When parents get older and turn to their adult children, this often involves a major set of role reversals for all parties. Parents had been responsible for their children, and now their children become responsible for them. Older persons, because of different levels of ability, find themselves in different relationships with their children. But ultimately the older persons give much less than they receive when they depend on their adult children, because their decreased resources limit what they can give.

Many older people in the United States live with their children. About one-third of all elderly adults who have living children live with them. Such joint households are usually two-generational, not three-generational households, with children in them. Usually the middle-age couples have one of their parents move in with them after their own children grow up and leave home. This kind of family is different from the common model because it is made up of elderly and middle-age adults.

Elderly adults move in with children when there are few other options; for example, when there is not enough money to live alone, when the parent's health is so poor that self-help is impossible, or, to a lesser extent, when the elderly person is widowed. In general, this is not a move older people will make if there are any other possible options.

When elderly people move in with their adult children, the reasons and the definitions can make a great deal of difference in the satisfaction of the living arrangement. When it is the choice of all, this is related to a higher level of overall satisfaction with life. But when it is seen as an obligation, satisfaction is reduced for all concerned.

The amount of interaction between older people and their children is not an accurate measure of satisfaction between them. High interaction between older persons and their adult children may be based on a feeling of obligation rather than any strong, positive emotional bonds. Sometimes a high rate of contact between elderly parents and their children is largely symbolic and ritualistic. It is carried out as a sense of duty and not as a result of interpersonal desire.

A study by Woods and Robertson found no positive relationship between frequency of contact with children and higher morale among older people. In fact, in some cases there was evidence of an inverse relationship between frequency of contact and morale. "There is the possibility that frequent contact and aid between older people and their children may be largely ritualistic, based on obligation which is devoid of warmth and closeness."[2]

Adult children may reject their elderly parents and deliberately avoid contact with them. A 79-year-old widow said:

> My two children don't see very much of me. One lives out in California and I fly out to see them for a week every year. That takes care of their responsibility to me and I know they don't really enjoy my visit. My son lives only a mile away and I don't see him more than twice a year. They have their own lives and they don't need me around. But I do have my friends and one thing we have in common is that several of them have children that treat them in the same way as mine.

But whatever the type of relationship, as people get older their interaction and activity with other people decline. A pervasive fact of life for the older person is the loss of relationships. This can be the loss of spouse, family, and friends through death and the loss of colleagues through retirement. Also, the nature of the relationships changes with age, so the functions often change. Increasingly the relationship may become one of dependency by the aging person on another.

The norms that govern kinship have lapsed or changed in a variety of ways that make them closer to those of friendship. In part this is because the power of kinship ties has been greatly reduced. Basically the difference between kinship patterns of the past and the present is that today being related to a person is often not enough. Kin require that something be achieved in the relationship—that it become a friendship as well as kinship. And sometimes a kin relationship may be allowed to wane or die out in an interpersonal sense, as can happen with friendship.

Today among older persons close relationships with a variety of relatives continue. One study of older people found that 15 percent of those who were named as friends were also relatives. And sometimes the reverse is true—when friends are labeled and dealt with as pseudo-kin. Sometimes certain friends are defined as having the characteristics typical of kin, and vice versa.[3]

But many older people continue to believe that the only close and meaningful relationships can and should be with kin. A 70-year-old woman said:

> My children and grandchildren spend time with me so I don't need any friends. Anyway, blood is thicker than water. Most of the folks I know my age only want to talk about their own kids. They don't really want to hear about mine—and I guess that's fair. With your own family you feel comfortable and that's the way I prefer it.

Research in recent years shows that friendship for older people is important. For example, one national study found that most social life at all ages is with friends. For those persons over age 65 who have friends, 91 percent see those friends almost every day. "This percentage is not significantly lower than the 94 percent of younger people who see their friends all the time."[4]

At all ages having ties that are emotionally satisfying is important. A purely objective relationship between individuals can be difficult because it is detached from human feelings. "It is a relationship that by definition creates distance, loneliness, and estrangement, and which can, at its worst, permit completely inhumane actions."[5] It is this kind of cold relationship that many older people are confronted with in medical care, their living facilities, and contact with governmental agencies. Therefore, the closeness of friendship and kin are often important as a means of easing those impersonal relationships.

Similarity of age is a major characteristic of most friendships, and this is especially true among the elderly. The similarity of age puts them in such common situations as being retired or widowed. And having lived over the same period of time, they usually have a similar value, interests, and experiences. It has been demonstrated that if older people have others their own age living near them, they will overwhelmingly develop friendships with those persons of their own age. One study found that friendship patterns varied in direct proportion to the number of aged peers that lived nearby. "By and large the enriched and age-segregated environment had produced positive effects in the lives of older residents. It promoted social involvement and enhanced morale and self image."[6]

Another study found that when the elderly live among other old people, their friendships and interactions with neighbors increase greatly. These elderly had more friends, saw them more often, and showed a higher level of social activity.

> Hence, people are unequivocally integrated into friendship groups to the extent that they have older neighbors who effectively constitute their potential friendship field. Furthermore, the larger the potential field, the less likely are the older people to have younger friends.[7]

Montgomery found that levels of interaction and morale were significantly higher among those who lived in age-homogeneous settings than among those who lived in age-heterogeneous settings. This was because the similarity of age provided many opportunities to develop friendships with people like themselves. A normative system also developed that helped facilitate adjustment to old age.[8] In such a system all share the common factor of old age and therefore have the means of socially and psychologically supporting and helping one another.

As many older people move into various kinds of retirement villages, disagreements have arisen about the effects of such an environment on their lives. Some have argued that isolating the elderly from younger people had a negative effect. But according to Montgomery, the research seems to tip the scale in favor of age-concentration living areas.

> Those environments appear to increase the number of friends and the extent of social interaction, to increase morale, and to contribute to a normative system in which the aged are spared competition and possibly conflict with the life styles of younger persons.[9]

One reason why living in an age-homogeneous environment is so important is that the older person has fewer opportunities to make friends than he or she did in the past. The number and type of friendships open to an individual at various stages of life depend less on age than on the other roles he or she plays. As the total cluster of roles change over the years, friendship relations and their possibility of development are effected. For example, retirement removes work as a source of friendship. This may make the neighborhood more important.

As people get older there may be new problems with friendships. One study of Americans over age 65 found evidence of shallowness of friendships, although there was frequently loneliness and a desire for more intimate relationships. The problem often was a recurrent expression of mistrust about new relationships. Often, aging brings with it a resistance and concern with things that are new. Therefore, the potential of new friendships may be viewed with apprehension. DuBois observes that "the aging process brings with it certain inescapable frustrations which makes an easy and rewarding friendship, which the young may enjoy, a major problem in both social and individual adjustment for the elderly."[10]

But for many there is the problem of finding new friends to replace, at least in part, those who have been lost through the ending of work and marriage. They seek those who share their needs, interests, and experiences. It is peer friendship, not filial relationships, that basically determine morale in old age.

Lowenthal and Haven found a clear and consistent relationship between social resources and good morale, and low social interaction was strongly related to depression. The presence of a confidante was positively related to indicators of adjustment. The absence of a confidante was related to low morale.[11]

The above study found that among men, morale deteriorated evenly with advancing age, from about one-third "depressed" among those under 65 to about three-fifths among those 75 and older. By contrast, the youngest women were more depressed than the youngest men, but there was no increase as they got older. In fact, there was a slight decrease in depression among the older women. In this study the importance of confidantes for both sexes was very important. The majority of those who had lost a confidante were depressed, while the majority of those who maintained confidantes were satisfied.[12]

SEX DIFFERENCES IN FRIENDSHIPS

One study found that women age 60 to 64 had nearly half again as many friends as did men of the same age. It also appears that lower-class men have the fewest friends of all. Those men may hold to a concept of verility which discourages the development of types of intimacy with women other than the purely sexual. "Thus, with the waning of sexual potency or the loss of a partner with advanced age, they are left with fewer alternatives for an intimate relationship than are women."[13]

Powers and Bultena found that sex differences in friendships extended into late life and that friendships were more extensive and meaningful for women than for men. The older men relied more on wives for intimacy, while the women more often turned to friends of the same sex for intimacy and affection. The older women were also more likely to turn outside the family for emotional support; and if they lost a close friend, they usually established new relationships. "It may be that for men intimate ties in late life are related to the loss of certain basic resources–a spouse, income, job and health."[14] Often it is men's problems that lead them to seek interpersonal relationships. The Powers-Bultena study also found that men were more likely to have never had an intimate friend. About two-thirds of the men and one-third of the women did not currently have a close friend and had never lost one. About one-half of the men and nearly three-fourths of the women who had lost a close friend were involved in another intimate friendship.[15]

Powers and Bultena's respondents were 70 years of age and older. The men had a significantly higher amount of interaction than did the women. This difference in overall interaction was a function of both the number of persons within the interactional network and the frequency of contact between those who interacted. Males' contact with their children and families was half again as high as females' contact, and their interaction with spouses and friends was twice as high. "Women had significantly higher contact with one category of interactants–intimate friend. Intimate friends contributed nearly as much to the total interactional scores of women as did spouses."[16] Friends serve a somewhat different function for older women than older men. The men were not likely to have intimate friends for social and emotional support in late life except when they experienced the loss of other resources.[17]

Another study came to conclusions similar to that by Powers and Bultena. It found that males over 70 claimed to have more social contacts than did females. But when the contacts of the men were examined closely, they were often found to be restricted to the men's wives, children, and children's families. But generally, the men were less likely to have intimate friends than were the women. Furthermore, "although fathers may claim strong ties with their children, the kinship ties are much weaker than those women have with their daughters."[18]

Generally, the social worlds of aged men and women are different in a variety of ways. Men may have more frequent social contact, but their interaction is limited to family and a few friends. And the men are less likely than women to have intimate friends and also less likely to replace lost friends. "Women have a diverse social world and many have intimate ties outside the immediate family."[19] Whatever friendships older men and women have, they are overwhelmingly limited to the same sex. Powers and Bultena found that less than one-tenth of the friendships of women and one-third of those of men were with the opposite sex.[20] The sex differences are largely a result of the different life expectancies for men and women: far fewer men are available with whom the older woman can develop friendships.

RETIREMENT

The main adult role for the American middle-class male is that of his occupation. He typically spends over 40 years working, which often ends abruptly with retirement. Over the years he makes friends on the job, but he may also have experienced the contradictions of friendship and work—the force of competition which makes friendship difficult and sometimes even impossible. In general, positive attitudes to work over the years have been linked to the development of friendships in that setting.

When retirement occurs, often retirees lose their primary source of friendships. This leads to reliance on other social agencies for the development of friendships. The familiar setting of the retired man's neighborhood is not a good source of friends—generally, if it was not before retirement, it will not be after retirement. The proliferation of clubs for the aged is evidence that the traditional settings of work, family, and neighborhood are no longer effective for many retirees.

For most men who retire, the change is a sharp one; they do not make a gradual transition. Often literally, they are at work one day and gone the next. Berado found that retirement removed a man from his occupational peer group and either drastically reduced or completely eliminated his participation in those informal but meaningful social relations developed in the job. He goes on to point out that in contrast "the death of the spouse, on the other hand, eliminates only a single crucial social relationship."[21]

Retirement, in removing the man from the work world, leaves him with a sense of loss and isolation. A 68-year-old retired man said:

> What I miss the most since I retired are the men I worked with. They were my friends. Other than a couple who are friends with the wife and me, I have no friends now. I went back to the shop a couple of times after I retired–but it wasn't the same. So I guess I don't have any friends anymore.

Retirement thus means the loss of not only the job but also the interpersonal relationships linked to it. Daily interaction with friends ends. The retired man who returns to work can only be a visitor and quickly discovers that the work world continues without him. The shared interests and concerns that supported his friendships with his fellow workers receive less reinforcement. This is especially true when the friend remains at work and continues to have work-related experiences the retiree can no longer share. "Whether work-based friendships will survive retirement may depend heavily upon whether alternative bases for shared experiences exist or can be developed."[22]

Blau found that the retired man often experiences not only loneliness but also self-denigration. The loss of his work and social relationships leads him to question the very meaning of his existence. And he often feels regret–that in the past he had failed to cultivate other interests besides his work. "Thus he has neither resigned himself to his difficulties nor has he been able to resolve them. And his inability to do so gives him a sense of inadequacy–'there is something wrong with me.' "[23]

Retirement affects the social life of individuals in other ways. It is sometimes difficult for the elderly to adjust their married lives to the drastic changes in the standard of living they usually must make. This sometimes results in difficulty in maintaining satisfactory ties with relatives, friends, and community organizations. They can no longer afford to do many of the things they once could, and this may limit their activities with friends.

However, retirement is not always a negative experience. One study found no evidence of mounting or increased health problems after retirement. In fact, a fairly substantial number of retirees subjectively perceived their health as improved after their retirement. And there are "several studies which support the contention that health does not fail markedly after retirement and in a substantial number of retirees it actually improves."[24]

ISOLATION IN OLD AGE

With the loss of relatives and friends, with retirement from work, and with more limited physical mobility, old age for many can mean increased isolation. One study found that although elderly women have a greater chance of being socially isolated than men, when an older man is socially isolated he is more likely than an older woman to be extremely isolated.[25]

For almost all human beings there is a need at all ages to interact with others. For the most part, on many occasions, people simply need each other. Lynch points out that this is true even though in recent years many people try to console themselves with such cliches as "I'm OK so you must be OK" while all the time they are not "OK." Often feelings of isolation are massaged with slogans that only serve to make people all the more lonely. "In a conspiracy of silence about their true loneliness, people deceive each other, and so make loneliness and isolation all the more prevalent."[26]

However, some appear able to be lifelong isolates without particularly suffering. For example, Lowenthal and Haven found that lifelong isolates tend to have average or better morale and to be no more prone to hospitalization for mental illness in old age than anyone else. But in that study the happiest and healthiest were the elderly people with one or more close personal relationship.[27]

Isolation for the elderly in the city is often closely related to fear. One study discovered among white elderly persons, of whom many were living alone in poverty areas of the inner city, high levels of fear. The incidence of living alone was particularly high in the case of women "residing in a changing neighborhood, often among hostile neighbors whom they cannot understand, [where] there is considerable fear of crime and of person's different from one's self."[28] The elderly often feel both psychologically and socially alienated.

Loneliness for the elderly can be the result of a variety of factors. A very real one is the geographical dispersal and the death of friends and members of the family. Each time someone close is lost, this calls for rearrangements of activities in life to try to restore equalibrium. Often the aging person who loses someone close searches for a substitute but finds there are no candidates. There is no replacement of family and no bidding to become new friends.

Many people reaching old age are destined to be lonely. This loneliness can take a variety of forms. Loneliness can come from living in "aged" communities, from retirement, or from the loss of friends or a spouse. It is basically an inevitable result of a society that teaches its members from childhood that old people are for the most part irritable, worthless, and strange. "It is no wonder that the young treat the old with callousness and that the old regard the young with suspicion and anger. Nor is it astonishing that the old regard each other as senile, troublesome, and useless."[29]

Kivett found that rural living and widowhood pose a double threat to the quality of the older woman's life. Three out of four older rural widows experienced varying degrees of loneliness, for which there was no single cause. Even frequent interaction with children, peers, and others did not necessarily correlate with decreased loneliness. Rural widows perceiving themselves as in poor health and tied down because of transportation difficulties were showed more likely to express loneliness.[30]

Today many of the needs of the elderly are met through the impersonal bureaucracy of government services. It is the government that provides the basic services for older people in such important areas as financial support, health, and transportation. Of course, family and friends retain considerable importance, particularly in meeting the unique needs of the given individual. The evidence is strong that "an older person without a circle of significant others can be severely disadvantaged."[31]

With aging the world of elderly persons shrinks. They often become physically limited in mobility. It is estimated that persons over 65 years of age spend 70 to 90 percent of their lives in their home environment. Of all people, only very small children, the chronically ill, and those in prisons are so bound by where they live. And for the aged with physical illnesses, the space restrictions become even tighter. "Indeed, for the enfeebled and the ill, life space is reduced to a house or an apartment, to a room and ultimately to a bed within the four restrictive walls."[32]

While the health of most older people is good, nevertheless at some point almost all have some health problems. When this happens the individual needs others not only for physical care but also for psychological support. For example, studies of coronary patients show they desperately need not only medical support but also the support of family and friends even long after they leave the hospital. Some studies suggest that the most serious medical problems occur after the patient leaves the hospital: he or she may have regained physical and psychological strength in the hospital but may feel deserted and lonely on returning home. A special problem in convalescence and in cases of chronic disability "is the lack of contact with friends and neighbors."[33]

Lynch estimates that up to one-third of all patients who have had heart attacks fail to return to work not because of medical problems but rather because of psychological difficulties. Whatever their reasons for failing to return to work, they often develop greater social isolation, loneliness, and depression.[34]

The care some elderly people need as a result of illness may be met through caretaking institutions. Often residential change required for the elderly, especially if it involves movement into some kind of caretaking institution, involves high costs. This move is often related to a higher probability of death, or a decline in physical health and psychological well-being.[35] Homes for the elderly are often seen as places to go to die.

For many elderly people who feel lonely or isolated, illness becomes a socially legitimate method for gaining attention. In fact, some lonely people experience important gains by getting ill. At least for a period of time during their hospitalization they receive compassionate support from the medical personnel. This may give them something that is missing in their lives—human attention. "The typical single, widowed, or divorced individual remains far longer in the hospital for the identical medical problems than do married people."[36]

BEREAVEMENT

Marriage is also linked to life expectancy. For example, for divorced, widowed, and single men, the overall death rates for cardiovascular disease are two to three times higher than for married men. For almost every other major cause of premature death there is a marked increase for the nonmarried over the married. The differences in death rates may be as high as tenfold. And almost every type of "cancer is significantly influenced by marital status, with the widowed, divorced and single almost always having significantly higher death rates."[37]

Lynch also reports that men who had a myocardial infarction reported more frequent dissatisfaction with their marital life than did men in general. And men who reported they felt a lack of emotional support from their wives were far more likely to become attack victims. "It appears that the individuals who are supported by love and secure family and community bonds can cope much better with stressful psychological situations than individuals who are deprived of such support."[38]

Marriage can have even broader effects on the life of the individual. Marriage not only influences the heart itself but also affects other behaviors, such as eating, drinking, smoking, and general lifestyle, all of which can have an effect on health. A bad marriage can lead to all kinds of indulgences that are potentially dangerous to health. When people are under stress, they may not take care of themselves.

Often as people get older their marriages serve as protection against many potential problems. The couple may unite in fighting the outside enemies–illness, loneliness, and death. "The spector of death tends to keep people married, each to nurse the other during the final days. It is more often the woman who has the task of nursing her husband and then faces years of loneliness."[39] Grief is also a common companion of old age. And apathy and shock are common psychological results of the death of close friends and relatives. Furthermore, physical disease and social isolation sometimes accompany or follow the bereavement of a spouse or a friend.

The sudden loss of a loved one can abruptly remove human companionship and the major source of love and caring from one's life. Loneliness and grief often overwhelm bereaved individuals, taking a severe toll on their health. "As the mortality statistics indicate, this is no myth or romantic fairytale–all available evidence suggests that people do indeed die of a broken heart."[40] A 72-year-old widow said:

> I felt so lost after my husband's death. I would wander around the empty house and cry. After our children had drown up my whole life was with my husband. It has been a year now and I still don't

want to see much of my friends. There can be no replacement for him—I don't know what I am going to do.

Evidence shows that how the widow reacts to the death of her husband affects her sense of isolation. One study found that when the widows expressed high anger at their husbands' death, they became more socially isolated than those women whose anger was less severe. For the former, "whether they drove their friends and relatives away or whether they dealt with their angry feelings by shutting themselves up at home, the result was loneliness and insecurity."[41]

While after the death of their spouses some widows may turn to relatives and friends for support, many do not. For some women the death of the spouse ends that relationship against their will, and, as a result, they may willfully end other relationships. These are usually relationships which had significance only when shared with the deceased husband. It may also be that the grief sometimes makes persons unsure of their ability to relate to others, and as a result they withdraw. They may have been highly dependent on their husbands for social interaction with other people.

Berardo found that the death of the spouse was more likely to bring about the sense of being "old" if the aged person failed to participate in a friendship group.[42] If left on their own with no social supports, these elderly would dwell on their misfortune and see themselves in the more negative light of "old age." Being with others often helps block self-pity.

It seems that the development of a point of view about death requires some capacity to absorb the loss of one's close friends and relatives, as well as the capacity to accept one's own ultimate death. It may be that accepting the death of friends is even more difficult than accepting the notion of one's own death. This is because the death of peers destroys the social group to which the adult is a member. "Losing one's friends and relatives means a loss of daily companionship, a shared world of memories and plans, and a source of support about values and social norms."[43]

THE WIDOWER

The interest in the social adjustments of the widower have been less than for the widow because there are far fewer surviving older husbands. But there are some considerations for the older man who survives his wife that are different than for the older woman who survives her husband. Often retirement has made the man highly dependent on his wife for his personal meaning and social significance. Her death, then, results in an even greater sense of isolation from kin and community relations, which he had often depended on his wife to maintain. By contrast, the widow has a greater opportunity for role continuity; "housekeeping, interacting with relatives, going to church, and participating in various other kinds of formal and informal relationships."[44]

Berardo found that with regard to sex differences among persons under 70, the loss of a spouse had a more adverse effect on the social participation of widowers than on that of widows. In part this was because the aged widower occupied a more deviant position than his female counterpart. Most of the friends of the widower in his sixties are still married and, because of women's greater life expectancy, there are going to be far fewer widowers.[45]

The elderly widower is less likely to have relatives living in the community and less likely to belong to various social organizations. While the widow may be able to find meaningful alternatives in other types of social relationships, effective substitution for the loss of a spouse appears to be harder for the widower.[46]

In comparison to persons in other marital statuses, in the Berardo study widowers were least likely to be living with their children or to have any high degree of interaction with kin that provided them with satisfying family relationships. They were also less likely to have friends either inside or outside the community or to be satisfied with their opportunities to be with close friends. "Further, they were the least likely to be church members, or to attend church services, or to belong to and participate in formal organizations or groups."[47]

When the elderly widower seeks out social relationships, he must turn to friends because he has fewer kinship ties than do widows. One study found that among males, 44 percent of the widowers indicated friendship interaction "all the time" as compared with only 16 percent of the aged married men with living spouses. Among the women in the study, 37 percent of the widows versus 26 percent of the women whose husbands are alive maintained friendship interaction at the highest level.[48] Another study concluded that extensive association with friends became an important mechanism of adjustment to old age for the widower.[49]

In general, being a widower has more negative social consequences than does being a widow. The elderly female is more likely to be closely supported by relatives, since the maintenance of kin networks has depended more heavily on females than on males. But more than that, the elderly widow is more likely to maintain memberships in formal organizations and to continue to participate in these and other meaningful associations. "Widowhood, in old age, particularly among males, is therefore often characterized by unhappiness, low morale, mental disorders, high death rates, and high suicide rates."[50]

There is also some evidence that the long-range effects of bereavement after the loss of one's spouse are greater for the widower than for the widow. Parkes found that the widow showed more overt distress after bereavement than did the widower, and that the widows' psychological and social adjustment a year after the death of their husbands was not as good than that of the widowers. However, at two to four years after bereavement, it was the men who were found to have taken longer to recover than the women.[51] While the shock of death may be greatest for women, it may be that in the long run adjustment to coping with life as a widowed person is more difficult for the man.

The greater suicide rates among widowers is the most dramatic evidence of their greater problems in coping with life. Bock and Webber found that elderly widowed males were more likely to commit suicide than were men with living spouses, not just because they had lost a significant role partner but also because they were isolated in many other ways—from kin, friends, neighbors, and formal organizations.[52] Bock further found that marriage alone was not enough to prevent suicide. The preventing of suicide was greatly increased by involvement in other social groups. "Thus, married males who had no relatives in the county or who belonged to no organizations displayed a suicide rate higher than the married males who had these other kinds of social bonds."[53]

In general, the higher suicide rates among the elderly are a result of their relatively greater loss of various kinds of external restraints, and these losses are most common for widowers. These are the losses of marital and occupational roles, as well as the loss of interaction with friends, relatives, and spouses. Widowers' increasing isolation perhaps has been related to and aggravated by increasing physical and economic difficulties. It was also found that the highest suicide rates were found at the lowest class level. This was explained "by the fact that lower class individuals were less likely to be married, to have relatives in the community, or to belong to community organizations."[54]

WIDOWS

Among elderly women who have lost their husbands, the routines of daily life are less disturbed and altered than for elderly widowers. The household tasks for the most part are the same. From this point of view, for a "large proportion of widows who live alone, daily household tasks constitute a very important variety of meaningful activity and ability to maintain certain standards of good housekeeping."[55]

The loss of a husband often means a reduction in kin relationships. Kin interaction for the elderly declines with the death of the spouse. The loss of the spouse often leads to the ending—or at least inhibition—of social bonds with in-laws. The widowed, when compared with married individuals, typically have a smaller number of kin with whom they may interact. Widows are more isolated than married individuals and have fewer close friend relationships.[56]

Evidence from a variety of studies suggests that the death of the elderly spouse constrains social relationships, and this leads to increased social deprivation for the widow. Lopata found that after the death of the husband the social contacts of the widow diminished. This was because of changes in the lifestyle of the widow and her friends, residential dispersion, lack of transportation, and strains developing in various relationships.[57]

For the widow, remarriage as a means of a new and significant interpersonal relationship is often not a realistic alternative. Among women over 50, widowhood usually is a permanent status, although not necessarily a role they prefer. Only five percent who become widowed after age 55 ever remarry. This is in sharp contrast to widowers, most of whom remarry if they are under 70. These differences in remarriage rates for widows and widowers (1) the greater number of widows providing more potential mates for widowers, and (2) the fact that men can, with far greater social approval, marry younger women.

As I suggested, contact with kin is often less for the widow than for women with living spouses. One study found that if the elderly widow lived alone and her kin lived more than several hours away, she was less likely to visit them than would a married couple of the same age. This meant there was less opportunity for her to become involved in family activities. Social activity was higher for married elderly than those elderly no longer married, especially if they lived alone.[58]

The importance of contact with the family for the elderly widow is subject to questioning. A study of widows found that respondents with children living nearby had morale no higher than that of respondents who either had no living children or had none who lived nearby. "Similarily, the frequency of contact with children has no significant association with morale."[59] This study went on to say that involvement with children did not seem to be an effective substitute or compensation for the lack of neighbors and friends. "These findings support the conclusion that family and neighboring are separate domains of involvement. Further, it reinforces the observation that family relationships are quite problematic for those elderly widows."[60]

With increasing age comes the end of all types of interpersonal relationships. Long-time acquaintances and friends die. And the fact of being a widow makes it difficult to engage in couple-oriented activities. Friendships that were based on the shared interests of a workplace have ended. There is increased difficulty in driving a car, managing airports, and walking distances, which limits contact with friends who live some distance away. Often all that is left is one's immediate neighborhood, and that may not always be satisfactory as a source of companionship.

But for the elderly, their friends often offer them something they cannot get from their families. Family ties are often characterized by a dissimilarity of experiences and an unequal exchange of aid. But friends normally relate to one another through common interests and generally are equal in their ability to exchange assistance. They are therefore usually able to avoid the psychological consequences of emotional and material dependency.[61]

While friendships are important for the elderly widow, they may still be lost or may not have existed for some women. Lopata found that 16 percent of the widows she studied said they had no friends in the year prior to their husbands' illness and at the time of the study still had none. Another 7 percent defined their past as lacking friends, although they had made friends since widowhood. "Thirty-eight percent list old friends but no new ones, leaving 39 percent with both old and new close associates."[62]

For the widows in Lopata's study, one in six were friendless. Sometimes these were women who did not consider friendship an important part of their lives. They were basically family oriented and did not attempt to develop any friendships. Another group of widows were aware of the possibility of friendships but did not have the self-confidence and social skills needed to develop such relationships. It was also found that the friendless women were most likely to have an eighth-grade education or less. "The presence of both old and new friends increases as soon as we reach high school graduates."[63]

Lopata further found that at the time of her study widows had fewer friends than before the death of their husbands. She suggests that the relative scarcity of new friends may be due to any one, or a combination of, four facts: (1) The recent occurrence of widowhood means they have not had time enough to develop new friends. (2) Women tend to develop friendships early in life. (3) Married women depend on couple-companionate interaction not available in widowhood. (4) There is an absence of social roles which ensure continued contact leading to increasing intimacy.[64]

Overwhelmingly, the friends of elderly widows are other widows or married women. Because of the greater life expectancy of women, there are far fewer men with whom they could be friends. In the Chicago-area study, almost 75 percent of the old friends and 81 percent of the new friends of the widows were women. Their male friends were husbands of the female associates or partners of couple friendships that had existed when their husbands had been alive.[65]

Among the elderly there may continue to be some jealousy

across sex lines that makes cross-sex friendship difficult. A 78-year-old widow said:

> I have my own ground floor apartment where I live alone. Most of the people who live there are senior citizens. A couple moved in next door a few months ago. They are in their early 70s. I found that often when I went out on my patio the man would come out and talk to me. He was pleasant and I enjoyed it. Before long his wife started to join us and it was clear that she didn't think much of his visiting me. She wasn't interested in being friends with me and she wanted to make sure he didn't either.

As was discussed in Chapter 1, it is common for persons who have close friendship ties to also have close kinship ties. This appears to be a characteristic of the elderly. One study found that those older people with strong family ties were just as likely to be integrated into a friendship network as were those elderly who had no family or infrequent contact with relatives.[66] For many elderly, their friendships exist along with family ties and not in place of ties that are missing.

Also of importance in comparing relationships between kin and friends are feelings of dependency. Dependency often makes satisfactory family relationships difficult, and this contributes to the limited morale gained from those ties. By contrast, "friends and neighbors are a good source of companionship since interaction with them proceeds on a more reciprocal basis." Arling and Blehar also found that the "personal morale" of the widow was related more strongly to the number of friends she had and to the amount of neighboring she engaged in than to family involvement. "Friendship and neighboring in turn were associated with the number and variety of daily activities widows engaged in, such as shopping, attending meetings, taking walks, etc."[67]

In her Chicago-area study, Lopata found that very few women turned to their friends in time of crisis or obtained their feelings of usefulness, independence, self-sufficiency, or security from allegedly intimate associates. "Most of the old friendships and even many of the new ones developed in widowhood never actually penetrate into the emotional support systems sufficiently to warrant first listing."[68] However, old age for these women did not bring increased services from siblings or other relatives. And their in-laws appeared infrequently in their support systems. These widows were, by choice or force of circumstances, relatively independent women.[69]

Other studies suggest the great importance of close ties for the elderly widow. This appears to be true whether the confidante relationships reflect the capacity and need for intimacy or whether they serve as a substitute for lost social contacts. The absence of close ties should be a factor in depression and low morale. "An intimate tie, then, may buffer the potential demoralization of widowhood, lessened social participation and retirement."[70]

Another option is available to some widows to provide them with social involvement—their participation in organized religion. It appears that widows are more likely to interact in religious organizations than are either widowers or married persons with living spouses. One study found that the widowed, as a group, may not be as isolated from their kin and friend social networks as other research has indicated. "Moreover, interaction in religious organizations, particularly for widows, is pronounced and perhaps serves as a surrogate 'family.' "[71]

As was suggested, neighbors can be very important to the widow. Arling and Blehar found that those elderly widows who had a number of neighbors they could visit and many friends in the neighborhood were the most likely to have someone in which they could confide. They were also the least likely to feel lonely, feel the most likely to be useful, and perceived the greatest community respect for elderly persons.[72]

Often the widow's loneliness comes to be part of her life. The loneliness can be associated with the death of the husband and withdrawal from others. Parkes found that despite their loneliness, only a few widows spent more time in social contact with friends and relatives than they had done before bereavement and a number of them said they spent less time in social contact. A number did not seek social relationships as a substitute for the companionship of their husbands.[73] Increased aloneness is often the widow's conscious choice.

NOTES

1. Lee, Gary R., "Marriage and Morale in Later Life," *Journal of Marriage and the Family,* February 1978, p. 137.
2. Woods, Vivian and Joan F. Robertson, "Friendship and Kinship Interaction: Differential Effect on the Morale of the Elderly," *Journal of Marriage and the Family,* May 1978, p. 368.
3. Ibid., p. 372.
4. Troll, Lillian E. et al., *Families in Later Life* (Belmont, CA: Wadsworth, 1979), pp. 6-7.
5. Lynch, James J., *The Broken Heart* (New York: Basic Books, 1977), p. 197.
6. Montgomery, James E., "The Housing Patterns of Older Families," *The Family Coordinator,* January 1972, p. 41.
7. Rosow, Irving, "Old People: Their Friends and Neighbors," *American Behavioral Scientist,* Sept.-Oct., 1970, p. 63.
8. Montgomery, "Housing Patterns of Older Families," p. 42.
9. Ibid., p. 42.
10. DuBois, Cora, "The Gratuitous Act: An Introduction to the Comparative Study of Friendship Patterns," in *The Compact,* E. Leyton, ed. (Canada: University of Newfoundland Press, 1974), p. 25.
11. Lowenthal, Majorie Fiske and Clayton Haven, "Interaction and Adaptation: Intimacy as a Critical Variables," *American Sociological Review,* February 1968, p. 25.
12. Ibid., p. 26.
13. Ibid., p. 30.
14. Powers, Edward A. and Gordon L. Bultena, "Sex Differences in Intimate Friendships of Old Age," *Journal of Marriage and the Family,* November 1976, p. 745.
15. Ibid., p. 743.
16. Ibid., p. 742.
17. Ibid., p. 745.
18. Tognoli, Jerome, "Male Friendship and Intimacy Across the Life Span," *Family Relations,* July 1980, p. 273.
19. Powers and Bultena, "Sex Differences in Intimate Friendships of Old Age," p. 746.

20. Ibid., p. 744.

21. Berardo, Felix, "Survivorship and Social Isolation: The Case of the Aged Widow," *The Family Coordinator,* January 1970, p. 16.

22. Hess, Beth, "Friendship," in *Aging and Society,* M. W. Riley, M. Johnson, and A. Foner, eds. (New York: Russell Sage Foundation, 1972), p. 365.

23. Blau, Zena Smith, *Old Age In A Changing Society* (New York: New Viewpoints, 1973), p. 4.

24. Garrity, Thomas F. and Martin B. Marx, "The Relationship of Recent Life Events to the Health of the Elderly," in *Dimensions of Aging: Readings,* J. Hendricks and C. D. Hendricks, eds. (Cambridge, MA: Winthrop, 1979), p. 104.

25. Tunstall, Jeremy, *Old and Alone* (London: Routledge and Kegan Paul, 1966), p. 83.

26. Lynch, *The Broken Heart,* p. 205.

27. Lowenthal and Haven, "Interaction and Adaptation," p. 20.

28. Hutchinson, Ira W., "The Significance of Marital Status for Morale and Life Satisfaction Among Lower-Income Elderly," *Journal of Marriage and the Family,* May 1975, p. 292.

29. Gordon, Suzanne, *Lonely in America* (New York: Touchstone, 1976), p. 193.

30. Kivett, Vira R., "Loneliness and the Rural Widow," *The Family Coordinator,* October 1978, p. 392.

31. Cantor, Marjorie H., "Effect of Ethnicity on Life Styles of the Inter-City Elderly," in Hendricks and Hendricks, *Dimensions of Aging,* p. 287.

32. Montgomery, p. 37.

33. Lynch, p. 114.

34. Ibid., p. 115.

35. Garrity and Marx, "Relationship of Recent Life Events to the Health of the Elderly," p. 106.

36. Lynch, p. 209.

37. Ibid., p. 43.

38. Ibid., p. 67.

39. Butler, Robert N., *Why Survive?* (New York: Harper and Row, 1975), p. 395.

40. Lynch, p. 56.

41. Parkes, Colin M., *Bereavement,* (Harmondsworth, England: Penguin, 1975), p. 105.

42. Berardo, "Survivorship and Social Isolation," p. 16.

43. Newman, B. M. and P. R. Newman, "Later Adulthood," in Hendricks and Hendricks, p. 129.

44. Bock, Wilbur E. and Irving L. Webber, "Suicide Among the Elderly: Isolating Widowhood and Mitigating Alternatives," *Journal of Marriage and the Family,* February 1972, p. 29.

45. Berardo, p. 17.

46. Ibid., p. 29.

47. Ibid., p. 14.

48. Petrowsky, Marc, "Marital Status, Sex and the Social Networks of the Elderly," *Journal of Marriage and the Family,* November 1976, p. 752.

49. Blau, Zena Smith, "Structural Constraints on Friendship in Old Age," *American Sociological Review,* 1961, p. 430.

50. Bock, Wilbur E., "Aging and Suicide: The Significance of Marital, Kinship, and Alternative Relations," *The Family Coordinator,* January 1972, p. 73.

51. Parkes, *Bereavement,* p. 149.

52. Bock and Webber, "Suicide Among the Elderly," p. 25.

53. Bock, "Aging and Suicide," pp. 75-76.

54. Ibid., p. 77.

55. Berardo, p. 13.

56. Petrowsky, "Marital Status, Sex and the Social Networks of the Elderly," p. 750.

57. Lopata, Helena Znaniecki, *Women as Widows* (New York: Elsevier, 1979), p. 217.

58. Hildreth, Gladys J. et al., "Participation in and Enjoyment of Family Maintenance Activities by Elderly Women," *Family Relations,* July 1980, p. 389.

59. Arling, Greg, "The Elderly Widow and Her Family, Neighbors and Friends," *Journal of Marriage and the Family,* November 1976, p. 761.

60. Ibid., p. 763.

61. Ibid., p. 759.

62. Lopata, *Women as Widows,* p. 210.

63. Ibid., p. 212.

64. Ibid., p. 215.

65. Ibid., p. 214.

66. Arling, "The Elderly Widow and Her Family, Neighbors and Friends," p. 759.

67. Arling, Gregory and Mary Blehar, "Family and Friendship in Old Age," in *Families Today, Vol. I,* E. Corfman, ed. (Washington, DC: U.S. Department of Health, Education and Welfare, 1979), p. 187.

68. Lopata, p. 227.

69. Ibid., p. 363.

70. Powers and Bultena, p. 740.

71. Petrowsky, p. 756.

72. Arling and Blehar, "Family and Friendship in Old Age," p. 762.

73. Parkes, p. 123.

BIBLIOGRAPHY

Adams, Bert N., *Kinship in an Urban Setting.* Chicago: Markham, 1968.

Adams, Bert N., and James E. Butler, "Occupational Status and Husband-Wife Social Participation. *Social Forces,* June 1967, pp. 501-7.

Arling, Greg, "Resistance to Isolation Among Elderly Widows." *Aging and Human Development,* January 1976, pp. 67-86.

Albrecht, Stan L., "Correlates of Marital Happiness Among the Remarried." *Journal of Marriage and the Family,* November 1979, pp. 857-67.

Albrecht, Stan L., "Reactions and Adjustments to Divorce: Differences in the Experiences of Males and Females." *Family Relations,* January 1980, pp. 59-68.

Athanasiou, Robert and Gary A. Yoshioka, "The Spatial Character of Friendship Formation." *Environment and Behavior,* March 1973, pp. 43-65.

Babchuk, Nicholas, "Primary Friends and Kin: A Study of the Associations of Middle Class Couples." *Social Forces,* May 1965, pp. 483-93.

Babchuk, Nicholas and Alan P. Bates, "The Primary Relations of Middle-Class Couples: A Study in Male Dominance." *American Sociological Review,* Vol. 28, 1963.

Balswick, Jack, "The Inexpressive Male: Functional Conflict and Role Theory as Contrasting Explanations." *The Family Coordinator,* July 1979, pp. 331-36.

Banta, Thomas J. and Mavis Hetherington, "Relations Between Needs of Friends and Fiances." *Journal of Abnormal and Social Psychology,* Vol. 66, 1963, pp. 401-4.

Barnhart, Elizabeth, "Friends and Lovers in a Lesbian Counterculture Community," in Nona Glazer-Malbin, *Old Family/New Family Interpersonal Relationships.* New York: D. Van Nostrand Co., 1975, pp. 90-116.

Bates, Alan P., "Privacy–A Useful Concept?" *Social Forces,* Vol. 42, 1964, pp. 429-34.

Bell, Robert R. "Mateship in Australia: Some Implications for Female-Male Relationships." *LaTrobe University Working Papers,* No. 1. Melbourne, Australia: LaTrobe University, August 1973.

Bell, Robert R. "Swinging: Separating the Sexual from Friendship," in Nona Glazer-Malbin, *Old Family/New Family: Interpersonal Relationships.* New York: D. Van Nostrand Co., 1975, pp. 150-68.

Bell, Robert R., "Friendships of Women and Men." *Psychology of Women Quarterly,* Spring 1981.

Bensman, Joseph and Robert Lilienfeld, *Between Public and Private.* New York: Free Press, 1979.

Bequaert, Lucia H., *Single Women Alone and Together.* Boston: Beacon, 1976.

Berardo, Felix M., "Survivorship and Social Isolation: The Case of the Aged Widower." *The Family Coordinator,* January 1970, pp. 11-25.

Blau, Zena Smith, "Structural Constraints on Friendships in Old Age." *American Sociological Review,* 1961, pp. 429-39.

Bloom, Bernard, Stephen W. White, and Shirley J. Asher, "Marital Disruption as a Stressful Life Event," in George Levinger and Oliver C. Moles, *Divorce and Separation.* New York: Basic Books, 1979, pp. 184-200.

Bock, E. Wilbur, "Aging and Suicide: The Significance of Marital, Kinship and Alternative Relations." *The Family Coordinator,* January 1972, pp. 71-79.

Bock, E. Wilbur and Irving L. Webber, "Suicide Among the Elderly: Isolating Widowhood and Mitigating Alternatives." *Journal of Marriage and the Family,* February 1972, pp. 24-31.

Boissevan, J., *Friends of Friends.* Oxford, England: Basil Blackwell, 1974.

Booth, Alan, "Sex and Social Participation." *American Sociological Review,* April 1972, pp. 183-92.

Booth, Alan and Elaine Hess, "Cross-Sex Friendship." *Journal of Marriage and the Family,* February 1974, pp. 38-47.

Bott, Elizabeth, "Urban Families: Conjugal Roles and Social Networks." *Human Relations,* Vol. 8, 1955, pp. 345-84.

Bott, Elizabeth, *Family and Social Network.* London: Tavistock, 1957.

Bradney, Pamela, "Quasi-Familial Relationships in Industry." *Human Relations,* August 1957, pp. 271-79.

Brain, Robert, *Friends and Lovers.* New York: Basic Books, 1976.

Brenton, Myron, *Friendship.* New York: Stein and Day, 1975.

Brittain, Clay V., "Adolescent Choices and Parent-Peer Cross-Pressures," *American Sociological Review,* Vol. 28, 1963, pp. 385-91.

Buhler, Charlotte, "Loneliness in Maturity." *Journal of Humanistic Psychology,* Fall 1969, pp. 167-81.

Burns, Tom, "Friends, Enemies, and the Polite Fiction." *American Sociological Review,* December 1953, pp. 654-62.

Burridge, Kenel O. L., "Friendship in Tangu." *Oceana,* September 1956, pp. 177-89.

Campbell, Ernest Q. and C. Norman Alexander, "Structural Effects and Interpersonal Relationships." *American Journal of Sociology,* November 1965, pp. 284-89.

Centers, Richard, "Attitude Similarity-Dissimilarity as a Correlate of Heterosexual Attraction and Love." *Journal of Marriage and the Family,* May 1975, pp. 305-12.

Chambliss, William J., "The Selection of Friends." *Social Forces,* March 1965, pp. 270-80.

Chevan, Albert and J. Henry Korson, "The Widowed Who Live Alone: An Examination of Social and Demographic Factors." *Social Forces,* September 1972, pp. 45-53.

Chrisman, Noel J., "Situation and Social Network in Cities." *Canadian Review of Sociology and Anthropology,* Vol. 7, 1970, pp. 245-57.

Cohen, Yehudi A., "Some Aspects of Ritualized Behavior in Interpersonal Relationships." *Human Relations,* Vol. 11, 1958, pp. 195-214.

Colletta, Nancy Donohue, "Support Systems After Divorce: Incidence and Impact." *Journal of Marriage and the Family,* November 1979, pp. 837-46.

Copley, Frank O., *On Friendship and On Old Age.* Ann Arbor: University of Michigan Press, 1967.

Corwin, Ronald, Marvin J. Taves and J. Eugene Haas, "Social Requirements for Occupational Success: Internalized Norms and Friendship." *Social Forces,* December 1960, pp. 135-40.

Croog, Sydney H., Alberta Lipson, and Sol Levine, "Help Patterns in Severe Illness: The Roles of Kin Network, Non-Family Resources, and Institutions." *Journal of Marriage and the Family,* February 1972, pp. 32-41.

Curtis, James, "Voluntary Association Joining: A Cross-National Comparative Note." *American Sociological Review,* October 1971, pp. 872-80.

Curtis, Russell L. and Louis A. Zurcher, Jr., "Voluntary Associations and the Social Integration of the Poor." *Social Problems,* Winter 1971, pp. 339-57.

Curtis, Russell L., Jr., "Parents and Peers: Serendipity in a Study of Shifting Reference Sources." *Social Forces,* March 1974, pp. 368-75.

Day, Barbara R., "A Comparison of Personality Needs of Courtship Couples and Same-Sex Friendships." *Sociology and Social Research,* July 1961, pp. 435-40.

Denzin, Norman K., "The Significant Others of a College Population." *Sociological Quarterly,* Summer 1966, pp. 298-310.

Driberg, H. H., "The 'Best Friend' Among the Dianja." *Man,* Vol. 35, 1935, pp. 101-2.

DuBois, Cora, "The Gratuitous Act: Introduction to the Comparative Study of Friendship Patterns," in Elliott Leyton, *The Compact: Selected Dimensions of Friendship.* Canada: University of Newfoundland Press, 1974, pp. 15-32.

Duck, S., *Personal Relations and Personal Constructs: A Study of Friendship Formation.* New York: John Wiley, 1973.

Eder, Donna and Maureen T. Hallinan, "Sex Differences in Children's Friendships." *American Sociological Review,* April 1978, pp. 237-49.

Eisenstadt, S. N., "Friendship and the Structure of Trust and Solidarity in Society," in Elliott Leyton, *Thee Compact: Selected Dimensions of Friendship.* Canada: University of Newfoundland Press, 1974, pp. 138-45.

Epstein, Joseph, *Divorced in America.* New York: Penguin, 1974.

Feagin, Joe R., "A Note on the Friendship Ties of Black Urbanites." *Social Forces,* December 1970, pp. 303-8.

Floyd, H. Hugh, Jr., and Donald R. South, "Dilemma of Youth: The Choice of Parents or Peers as a Frame of Reference for Behavior." *Journal of Marriage and the Family,* November 1972, pp. 627-34.

Gibson, Geoffrey, "Kinship Family Network: Overheralded Structure in Past Conceptualizations of Family Functioning." *Journal of Marriage and the Family,* February 1972, pp. 12-23.

Glazer-Malbin, Nona, *Old Family/New Family: Interpersonal Relationships.* New York: D. Van Nostrand Co., 1975.

Glick, Paul C. and Graham B. Spanier, "Married and Unmarried Cohabitation in the United States." *Journal of Marriage and the Family,* February 1980, pp. 19-30.

Goode, William J., *After Divorce.* New York: Free Press, 1965.

Gordon, Michael and C. Edward Noll, "Social Class and Interaction with Kin and Friends." *Journal of Comparative Family Studies,* Autumn 1975, pp. 239-48.

Greeley, Andrew M., *The Friendship Game.* New York: Doubleday, 1971.

Hammond, Phillip E., Albert Gedlicks, Edward Lawler, and Louise Allen Turner, "Clergy Authority and Friendship with Parishers." *Pacific Sociological Review,* April 1972, pp. 185-201.

Hendricks, Jon, "Leisure Participation as Influenced by Urban Residence Patterns." *Sociology and Social Research,* July 1971, pp. 414-28.

Hendrix, Lewellyn, "Kinship, Social Networks, and Integration Among Ozark Residents and Out-Migrants." *Journal of Marriage and the Family,* February 1976, pp. 97-104.

Hepburn, John R., "Violent Behavior in Interpersonal Relationships." *Sociological Quarterly,* Summer 1973, pp. 419-29.

Hess, Beth, "Friendship," in Matilda White Riley, Marilyn Johnson, and Anne Foner, *Aging and Society, Vol. 3.* New York: Russell Sage Foundation, 1972, pp. 357-93.

Hutchinson, Ira W. III, "The Significance of Marital Status for Morale and Life Satisfaction Among Lower-Income Elderly." *Journal of Marriage and the Family,* May 1975, pp. 287-93.

Izard, Carroll E., "Personality Similarity and Friendship." *Journal of Abnormal and Social Psychology,* Vol. 61, 1960, pp. 47-51.

Ishino, Iwao, "The Oyabun-Kobun: A Japanese Ritual Kinship Institution." *American Anthropologist,* Vol. 55, 1953, pp. 695-707.

Jackson, Jacquelyne Johnson, "Comparative Life Styles and Family and Friend Relationships Among Older Black Women." *The Family Coordinator,* October 1972, pp. 477-85.

Kaufman, Debra Renee, "Associational Ties in Academe: Some Male and Female Differences." *Sex Roles,* Vol. 4, 1978, pp. 9-21.

Kempler, Hyman L., "Extended Kinship Ties and Some Modern Alternatives." *The Family Coordinator,* April 1976, pp. 143-49.

Key, William H., "Urbanism and Neighboring." *Sociological Quarterly,* Autumn 1965, pp. 379-85.

Kiefer, Thomas M., "Institutionalized Friendship and Warfare Among the Tausug of Jolo." *Ethnology,* July 1968, pp. 225-44.

Komarovsky, Mirra, *Blue Collar Marriage.* New York: Vintage Books, 1967.

Komarovsky, Mirra, "Patterns of Self-Disclosure of Male Undergraduates." *Journal of Marriage and the Family,* November 1974, pp. 677-86.

Kon, Igor S. and Vladimir A. Losenkov, "Friendship in Adolescence: Values and Behavior." *Journal of Marriage and the Family,* February 1978, pp. 143-55.

Kurth, Suzanne B., "Friendships and Friendly Relations," in George J. McCall, *Social Relationships.* Chicago: Aldine, 1970, pp. 136-70.

Lazarsfeld, Paul F. and Robert K. Merton, "Friendship as Social Process: A Substantive and Methodological Analysis," in Monroe Berger, Theodore Abel, and Charles H. Page, *Freedom and Control in Modern Society.* New York: Octagon Books, 1954, pp. 18-66.

Lee, Gary R., "Marriage and Morale in Later Life." *Journal of Marriage and the Family,* February 1978, pp. 131-39.

Levinger, George and Harold L. Raush, *Close Relationships.* Amherst: University of Massachusetts Press, 1977.

Lewis, Robert A., "Emotional Intimacy Among Men." *Journal of Social Issues,* Vol. 34, 1978, pp. 108-21.

Leyton, Elliott, *The Compact: Selected Dimensions of Friendship.* Canada: University of Newfoundland Press, 1974.

Little, Roger W., "Buddy Relations and Combat Performance," in Morris Janowitz, *The New Military.* New York: Russell Sage Foundation, pp. 195-224.

Litwak, Eugene, "Voluntary Associations and Neighborhood Cohesion." *American Sociological Review,* April 1961, pp. 258-71.

Litwak, Eugene and Ivan Szelenyi, "Primary Group Structures and Their Functions: Kin, Neighbors, and Friends." *American Sociological Review,* August 1969, pp. 465-81.

Loether, Herman J., "Propinquity and Homogeneity as Factors in the Choice of Best Buddies in the Air Force." *Pacific Sociological Review,* Spring 1960, pp. 18-22.

Lopata, Helena Znaniecki, "Couple-Companionate Relationships in Marriage and Widowhood," in Nona Glazer Melbin, *Old Family/New Family.* New York: D. Van Nostrand Co., 1975, pp. 119-49.

Lopata, Helena Znaniecki, "The Effect of Schooling on Social Contacts of Urban Women." *American Journal of Sociology,* Vol. 79, 1976, pp. 604-19.

Lopata, Helena Znaniecki, "Contributions of Extended Families to the Support Systems of Metropolitan Area Widows: Limitations of the Modified Kin Network." *Journal of Marriage and the Family,* May 1978, pp. 355-64.

Lopata, Helena Znaniecki, *Women as Widows.* New York: Elsevier, 1979.

Lowenthal, Majorie Fiske, "Social Isolation and Mental Illness in Old Age." *American Sociological Review,* February 1964, pp. 54-70.

Lowenthal, Margorie Fiske and Deeje Boler, "Voluntary vs. Involuntary Social Withdrawal." *Journal of Gerontology,* July 1965, pp. 363-71.

Lowenthal, Marjorie Fiske and Clayton Haven, "Interaction and Adaptation: Intimacy as a Critical Variable." *American Sociological Review,* February 1968, pp. 20-30.

Lynch, James J., *The Broken Heart.* New York: Basic Books, 1977.

McAllister, Donald J., Edgar W. Butler, and Edward J. Kaiser, "The Adaptation of Women in Residential Mobility," *Journal of Marriage and the Family,* May 1973, pp. 197-204.

McGahan, Peter, "The Neighborhood Role and Neighboring in a Highly Urban Area," *Sociological Quarterly,* Summer 1972, pp. 397-408.

McKinlay, John B., "Social Networks, Lay Consultation and Help-Seeking Behavior." *Social Forces,* March 1973, pp. 275-92.

Mayer, J., "The Self Restraint of Friends: A Mechanism of Family Transition." *Social Forces,* March 1957, pp. 230-40.

Malcolm, Arthur, "American Culture and the Phenomenon of Friendship in the Aged," in C. Tibbits and W. Donahue, *Social and Psychological Aspects of Aging.* New York: Columbia University Press, 1962, pp. 529-34.

Miller, Arthur A., "Reactions of Friends to Divorce," in Paul Bohannan, *Divorce and After.* New York: Doubleday, 1970, pp. 56-77.

Mirande, Alfred M., "Extended Kinship Ties, Friendship Relations, and Community Size: An Exploratory Inquiry." *Rural Sociology,* June 1970, pp. 261-66.

Naegele, Kasper D., "Friendship and Acquaintances: An Exploration of Some Social Dimensions." *Harvard Educational Review,* Vol. 25, No. 3, pp. 232-52.

Nagle, James A., "Power, Stability, and Friendships in Coalitions." *Pacific Sociological Review,* October 1973, pp. 519-37.

O'Brien, Patricia, *The Woman Alone.* New York: Quadrangle, 1973.

Otto, Luther B., "Girl Friends as Significant Others: Their Influence on Young Men's Career Aspirations and Achievements." *Sociometry,* September 1977, pp. 287-93.

Paine, Robert, "In Search of Friendship: An Exploratory Analysis in 'Middle Class' Culture." *Man,* December 1969, pp. 505-24.

Paine, Robert, "Anthropological Approaches to Friendship," in Elliott Leyton, *The Compact.* Canada: University of Newfoundland Press, 1974, pp. 1-14.

Palisi, Bartolomeo, "Ethnic Patterns of Friendship." *Phylon,* Fall 1966, pp. 217-25.

Parker, S. R. "Type of Work, Friendship Patterns, and Leisure." *Human Relations,* Vol. 17, 1964, pp. 215-19.

Parkes, Colin Murray, *Bereavement.* Harmondsworth, England: Penguin, 1975.

Parlee, Mary Brown, "The Friendship Bond." *Psychology Today,* October 1979, pp. 43-45, 49-50, 53-54, 113.

Petrowsky, Marc, "Marital Status, Sex, and the Social Networks of the Elderly." *Journal of Marriage and the Family,* November 1976, pp. 749-56.

Phillips, Derek L., "Social Participation and Happiness." *American Journal of Sociology,* March 1967, pp. 479-88.

Piker, Steven, "Friendship to the Death in Rural Thai Society." *Human Organization,* Fall 1968, pp. 200-4.

Potter, Robert G., Jr., and John F. Kantner, "Social and Psychological Factors Affecting Fertility: XXVII. The Influence of Siblings and Friends on Fertility." *The Milbank Memorial Fund Quarterly,* July 1955, pp. 246-67.

Potter, Robert J., "Social Conversation Among Friends, Familiars and Strangers." *Rocky Mountain Social Science Journal,* Vol. 4, 1967, pp. 153-60.

Powers, Edward A. and Gordon L. Bultena, "Sex Differences in Intimate Friendships of Old Age." *Journal of Marriage and the Family,* November 1976, pp. 739-47.

Ramey, James, *Intimate Friendships.* New Jersey: Spectrum, 1976.

Reina, Ruben E., "Two Patterns of Friendship in a Guatemalan Community." *American Anthropologist,* February 1959, pp. 44-61.

Reisman, John M., *Anatomy of Friendship.* New York: Irvington, 1979.

Rieger-Shionsky, Hagith, "The Conceptualization of the Roles of a Relative, a Friend, and a Neighbour." *Human Relations,* Vol. 22, 1969, pp. 355-69.

Roberts, John M., "Kinsmen and Friends in Zuni Culture: A Terminological Note." *Palacio,* Vol. 72, 1965, pp. 38-43.

Robson, R.A.H., "The Effects of Different Group Sex Compositions on Support Rates and Coalition Formation." *Canadian Review of Sociology and Anthropology,* Vol. 8, 1971, pp. 244-62.

Rosow, Irving, "Old People: Their Friends and Neighbors." *American Behavior Scientist,* September-October 1970, pp. 59-69.

Rubin, Zick, *Children's Friendships.* Cambridge, MA: Harvard University Press, 1980.

Salloway, Jeffrey Colman and Patrick B. Dillon, "A Comparison of Family Networks and Friend Networks in Health Utilization Care." *Journal of Comparative Family Studies,* Spring 1973, pp. 131-42.

Schwartz, Ronald D., "The Crowd: Friendship Groups in a Newfoundland Outport," in Elliott Leyton, *The Compact.* Canada: University of Newfoundland Press, 1974, pp. 71-92.

Seiden, Anne M. and Pauline B. Bart, "Woman to Woman: Is Sisterhood Powerful?" in Nona Glazer-Malbin, *Old Family/New Family.* New York: D. Van Nostrand Co., 1975, pp. 189-228.

Selman, Robert L. and Anne P. Selman, "Children's Ideas About Friendship: A New Theory." *Psychology Today,* October 1979, pp. 71-72, 74, 79-80, 114.

Short, James F., Jr., Differential Association with Delinquent Friends and Delinquent Behavior." *Pacific Sociological Review,* Spring 1958, pp. 20-25.

Shulman, Norman, "Life-Cycle Variations in Patterns of Close Relationships." *Journal of Marriage and the Family,* November 1975, pp. 813-21.

Simon, Rita James, Gail Crotts, and Linda Mahan, "An Empirical Note About Married Women and Their Friends." *Social Forces,* June 1970, pp. 520-25.

Smith, Carole R., Lev Williams, and Richard H. Willis, "Race, Sex and Belief as Determinants of Friendship Acceptance." *Journal of Personality and Social Psychology,* January 1967, pp. 127-37.

Srivastava, S. K. "Patterns of Ritual Friendship in Tribal India." *International Journal of Comparative Sociology,* September 1960, pp. 239-47.

Sutcliffe, J. P. and B. D. Crabbe, "Incidence and Degrees of Friendship in Urban and Rural Areas." *Social Forces,* October 1963, pp. 60-67.

Suttles, Gerald D., "Friendship as a Social Institution," in George J. McCall, *Social Relationships.* Chicago: Aldine, 1970, pp. 95-133.

Temme, Lloyd V. and Jere M. Cohen, "Ethnic Differences in High School Friendship," *Sociology of Education,* Fall 1960, pp. 459-64.

Tiger, Lionel, "Sex-Specific Friendship," in Elliott Leyton, *The Compact.* Canada: University of Newfoundland Press, 1974, pp. 42-48.

Timms, Duncan W.G., "Occupational Stratification and Friendship Nomination: A Study in Brisbane." *Australian and New Zealand Journal of Sociology,* April 1974, pp. 32-43.

Tomeh, Aida K., "Birth Order and Friendship Associations." *Journal of Marriage and the Family,* August 1970, pp. 360-69.

Verbrugge, Lois M., "The Structure of Adult Friendship Choices." *Social Forces,* December 1977, pp. 576-97.

Vogel, Ezra F., "From Friendship to Comradeship: The Change in Personal Relations in Communist China." *The China Quarterly,* January-March 1965, pp. 46-60.

Weinberg, S. Kirson, "Primary Group Theory and Closest Friendship of the Same Sex," in Tamatsu Shibutani, *Human Nature and Collective Behavior.* Englewood Cliffs, NJ: Prentice-Hall, 1970, pp. 301-19.

Weiss, Robert S., *Marital Separation.* New York: Basic Books, 1975.

Williams, Robin M., Jr., "Friendship and Social Values in a Suburban Community: An Exploratory Study." *Pacific Sociological Review,* Spring 1959, pp. 3-10.

Woods, Vivian and Joan F. Robertson, "Friendship and Kinship Interaction: Differential Effect on the Morale of the Elderly." *Journal of Marriage and the Family,* May 1978, pp. 367-75.

Young, T. R. "The Chiner Mate: Single Sex Mating." *International Journal of the Sociology of the Family,* March 1972, pp. 72-79.

Zito, Jacquiline M., "Anonymity and Neighboring in an Urban High-Rise Complex." *Urban Life and Culture,* October 1974, pp. 243-63.

NAME INDEX

SUBJECT INDEX

ABOUT THE AUTHOR

ROBERT R. BELL is Professor of Sociology at Temple University, where he has taught since 1954. He was also Professor of Sociology at LaTrobe University (Melbourne, Australia), from 1975 to 1977. He is the author of textbooks on marriage and the family; the sociology of education, deviance, human sexuality, and social problems; as well as professional books and many articles in the fields of marriage and the family and human sexuality. His book *Marriage and Family Interaction* is currently in its fifth edition (first published in 1963). Dr. Bell has been active in the American Sociological Association's Family Section, the National Council on Family Relations, the Society for the Study of Social Problems, and the Groves Conference on the Family.